Hitmakers: How Brands Influence Culture

Modern brands are hitmakers. Knowing how to influence consumers through collaborations, merch, entertainment, brand codes, icons and other cultural products (and not through advertising) is a matter of strategy. In this book, world-renowned brand expert, Ana Andjelic, shows how modern brand strategy needs to be redefined as the strategy of cultural influence, how brands today influence culture, how brands should address audiences and how the new approach to cultural hitmaking works organizationally and operationally.

A cultural hit is an idea, content or entertainment that a large number of consumers pay attention to, share and talk about. Once cultural hits become market hits, by lifting brand popularity or driving product sales, they have a strong financial return for a company. Brands are motivated to start producing as many cultural hits as possible, and these new formats replace traditional brand marketing strategies.

In the book, Ana Andjelic clearly articulates the complexity of this modern brand building, and provides a set of practical examples and tools that can be used by brand strategists to produce a cultural hit.

Ana Andjelic is a global brand executive and author of *The Business of Aspiration* and has been recognized three times by Forbes for her CMO work. Ana specializes in building brand-driven modern businesses. Most recently, she was the Global Chief Brand Officer of ESPRIT, responsible for ESPRIT's new brand vision and repositioning strategy in Europe and market re-entry in the NA and APAC. Prior to ESPRIT, Ana led the successful rebrand of Banana Republic, resulting in 27% YoY comparable sales increase. Ana also held positions as the CMO of Mansur Gavriel and the Chief Brand Officer of Rebecca Minkoff, where she introduced the Female Founders Collective platform. She is also a sought-after expert source for leading business and mainstream press, including the *Wall Street Journal*, *Washington Post*, *Financial Times*, *Fast Company*, the *Guardian*, *Forbes*, and *Vogue*.

"It is no surprise that established and aspiring brand experts alike look to Ana for insight and inspiration. Her ability to distill cultural observations and translate them into a framework to approach brand building is a rare skill that can only be honed from years of experience like Ana has, and by maintaining an endless well of curiosity about the world around us. If you are stuck in the rut of the mundane, ineffective brand marketing, you've come to the right place."

Steve Dool, *Brand, Marketing and Communications Director*, Depop

"In today's world, only brands that align themselves with culture are destined for greatness. This book is essential reading to understanding how product can be infused with cultural meaning."

Eugene Rabkin, *Founder and Editor of StyleZeitgeist*

"Brands, and those that think they are a brand, are so obsessed with exposing the insides of the fashion business, the 'bts' guts and gore of how it works and reporting on its failures, it has lost sight of why it exists in the first place – what its job is, and importantly how to do it well. Ana astutely, sharply and frankly, for our own good, directs us with Quentin Tarantino precision. A necessary wake-up call and adrenalin shot to get us back to strategies and creative ideas that contribute to culture in a meaningful way rather than sucking it dry with banal and wasteful tactics."

Gill Linton, *Founder of Byronesque*

"Ana is one of the sharpest, most perceptive and truly strategic thinkers in fashion today. Bringing a broad cultural awareness to an industry increasingly driven by antiquated practices and profit margins, she returns fashion to its rightful place as both a catalyst and an indicator of societal change. In this book, Ana interprets the popular zeitgeist, as well as the wider cultural shifts that creates it, and translates it into precise, actionable business practices that would greatly benefit any fashion executive, while capturing the imagination of any fashion enthusiast."

Shira Carmi, *CEO of Altuzarra*

"No one quite connects the dots between marketing and culture like Ana Andjelic. Her writing has become a required reading for those operating on the cutting edge of marketing, because it identifies the cultural laws of gravity that underpin the trend cycles we see spinning across our feeds every day."

Thom Bettridge, *Vice President, Creative and Content,* SSENSE

"Once again, Ana Andjelic puts words and tools to the ever elusive business of translating a magical brand's life-force, and in a time when we need them more than ever."

Christene Barberich, *Writer/Founder of* A Tiny Apt, *Co-Founder of* Refinery29 *and a New York Times best-selling author*

"Ana Andjelic has become one of the most innovative thinkers in the lifestyle marketing space. She has a unique understanding of translating cultural movements into applicable marketing playbooks, like I have never seen before. Building an influential brand today is far more complex and fragmented than it used to be. As such, this book is essential reading for any marketer that wants to operate at the cutting edge."

David Fischer, *Founder of* Highsnobiety

Hitmakers

How Brands Influence Culture

ANA ANDJELIC

Routledge
Taylor & Francis Group

LONDON AND NEW YORK

Designed cover image: Santos, Virgilio, Dilone, Manuel and Barbu, Ion
Photo: Richard Phibbs

First published 2025
by Routledge
4 Park Square, Milton Park, Abingdon, Oxon OX14 4RN

and by Routledge
605 Third Avenue, New York, NY 10158

Routledge is an imprint of the Taylor & Francis Group, an informa business

British Library Cataloguing-in-Publication Data
A catalogue record for this book is available from the British Library

Library of Congress Cataloging-in-Publication Data
Names: Andjelic, Ana, 1976– author.
Title: Hitmakers : how brands influence culture / Ana Andjelic.
Description: Abingdon, Oxon ; New York, NY : Routledge, 2025. | Includes
    bibliographical references and index.
Identifiers: LCCN 2024031162 (print) | LCCN 2024031163 (ebook) |
    ISBN 9781032878713 (hardback) | ISBN 9781032874463 (paperback) |
    ISBN 9781003534907 (ebook)
Subjects: LCSH: Branding (Marketing)—Social aspects. | Brand name
    products—Social aspects. | Popular culture.
Classification: LCC HF5415.1255 .A493 2025 (print) | LCC HF5415.1255
    (ebook) | DDC 658.8/27—dc23/eng/20240822
LC record available at https://lccn.loc.gov/2024031162
LC ebook record available at https://lccn.loc.gov/2024031163

ISBN: 978-1-032-87871-3 (hbk)
ISBN: 978-1-032-87446-3 (pbk)
ISBN: 978-1-003-53490-7 (ebk)

DOI: 10.4324/9781003534907

Typeset in Dante and Avenir
by Apex CoVantage, LLC

Contents

Preface

A couple of days before this book was finished, creative director of Chanel, Virginie Viard, stepped down. The news broke almost in sync with the release of Chanel's financial results which, during Viard's tenure, climbed by 14.6% to $19.7 billion.

Viard's work was a commercial but not a critical success. Cathy Horyn, a fashion critic, noted, "Money isn't everything. With a house of Chanel's status, its extraordinary story, the executives and owners ought to be equally – and maybe more – concerned with creativity and newness."[1] A prominent cultural commentator agreed: "Chanel had to save face with regards to criticism. They are still old school, with values other than money. How it used to be before Arnault ruined the industry. He doesn't give a f—— that no one likes Dior runway. As long as the money rolls in. Chanel wants both critical and commercial praise."[2]

Modern brands, from fashion to entertainment to art to travel, turn culture into a superstar commodity. Brands and culture have always been closely intertwined; both are helping us make sense of what is happening in the world around us and our place within it. Culture is a story. Brands are stories, invented to give products they sell and services they offer a context and meaning. They are tools that we use to make sense of the world. If we buy Nike, we identify as athletes. If we date on Bumble, we put forward a certain set of values and preferences. If we stay at the Four Seasons, we signal our status and taste. When we wear or use a brand's product or services, we tell a story about ourselves.

Without stories, there would be no brands, and modern brands are narrative universes. A24, a famed independent film production and distribution company, gained initial notoriety through its memorable merch and now offers product collections stemming from their shows. Erewhon, an upscale Los Angeles grocery, is the cultural hub, a celebrity hangout, a health food mecca, and a fashion brand. Like Marvel Cinematic Universe, brands increasingly develop their own universes, with interconnected set of characters, self-referential storylines, sequels, remakes and reboots, and methodical rollouts in categories ranging from tourism to branding, film and television, gaming and fashion, and advertising and publishing, making it unnecessary for us to ever leave them.

The core premise of a narrative universe is a simple and clear brand promise. Each world is built around a single idea, which is repeated constantly and consistently. This one idea can generate others, but a world always needs to have an anchor – an archetype or a primary emotion. For Apple, it was creativity. For Disney, it's magic. For Amazon, it's convenience.

A narrative universe protects brands from having to "cut through the noise" and forcefully command consumer attention because it is made out of a lot of simultaneous signals. These simultaneous signals are the cultural products that brands make to tell their story: collaborations, merch, entertainment, content, events, archives, brand codes, etc. These cultural products are connected into a brand's cultural influence strategy: they aimed at subcultures and niches, they grow through cumulative advantage, are produced at scale and released quickly, and live or die in the real world. Brands make a lot of cultural products in the hope that some of them, placed in the right context and amplified through media, will become hits. Once synchronized, like crickets or lightbulbs, cultural hits create a frequency that resonates within culture.

Modern brands are hitmakers: their stories are vibrations strong enough for the culture to hear.

Ana Andjelic
New York City, June 2024

Notes

1   Horyn, C. (2024, June 7). Chanel needed a change. *The Cut*. https://www.thecut.com/article/chanel-needed-a-change.html

2   Comment shared in a private text exchange.

Introduction
Brands as hitmakers

Before 1999, the "Centurion Amex" was an urban legend. An invitation-only, no-limit titanium card did not exist. When American Express launched its Black Card, a cultural hit became a market hit.

Fifteen years prior, Michael Jordan received a ban from the NBA on his black-and-red Nike Air Jordan 1 sneakers. NBA historically mandated that sneakers worn on court have to be 51% white. Jordan kept wearing his sneakers for a $5,000 fine per game, paid for by Nike, throughout the entire season. Nike turned the ban into the – wait for it – "Banned" campaign. "On October 15, Nike created a revolutionary new basketball shoe. On October 18, the NBA threw them out of the game. Fortunately, NBA can't keep you from wearing them. Air Jordans. From Nike," the campaign said.[1] As of 2024, the Jordan brand brings $6.59 billion in revenue, or 13% of Nike's total sales.[2] (It took NBA until 2018 to remove all sneaker restrictions.) A cultural hit became a market hit.

DOI: 10.4324/9781003534907-1

A cultural hit is an idea, an item, an experience, or entertainment that a large number of consumers pay attention to, share and talk about. Once cultural hits turn into market hits, by lifting brand popularity or driving product sales, they yield a strong financial return for a company.

Modern brands are hitmakers. They are in the business of producing as many cultural hits as possible, and these new formats are increasingly replacing the traditional brand marketing strategies. Hitmaker brands command higher prices, capture greater market share, maintain advantage over competition, avoid commodification, and enjoy greater customer loyalty.

Brands used to influence culture mostly through their advertising on mass media like TV, print, billboards, or public relations. Today, they influence culture through the cultural products they create: merch, collaborations, archive reissues, product icons, aesthetics, styling, brand codes, graphic design, retail experiences and entertainment.

Hit-making is the strategy of cultural influence. In the post-mono culture, media, and retail, brands are pushed to operate like a portfolio of products and categories that target different niche audiences. Mass is achieved through aggregation of niches. By targeting its different audience segments, a brand creates many doors in and increases it hold on the market.

A portfolio approach addresses the fact that not all of the brand's cultural products will become hits. Cultural markets are known as "ambiguous markets" where success is random and unpredictable. Now-iconic *Fight Club* was originally a flop, and so was equally iconic *Blade Runner*, which, at the time of its release, barely made its budget. *Assassin's Creed* became a Netflix's top 10 hit seven years after its release.

Success in ambiguous markets is mostly a matter of cultural moments and moods. Humans are social animals, and they never make decisions in isolation from each other, their social media, streets they walk in, content they watch/listen/read, and images, products, and people they are surrounded by.

How aspirational or desirable people assess something to be is more influenced by pop culture than personal choice. Calvin Klein's Jeremy Allen White's ad was released three days before White's first Golden Globe's win, and at the beginning of the awards season, where his successful hit *The Bear* was nominated for the first time in multiple categories. The mood for the campaign was right – White plays an underdog in his show, the show itself was an underdog in the awards season, and White has been an underdog on the awards circuit. The ad was released at the right cultural moment, but even then, it may have note become a hit (what if White didn't win?).

To turn some of its cultural products into hits, brands need to create a lot of them. This is a matter of creative production and media amplification. When ideas are tested in the real world, the creative, organizational, and operational balance shifts from strategy to execution, and from a couple of big ideas to a lot of smaller ones. The job of media is to amplify the cultural products that show early promise in terms of audience pick-up. Cultural products and media amplification always go together: without media amplification, cultural products would stay niche; without cultural products, media is just increasing click-through rates without creating cultural influence.

Media amplification of cultural influence is a creative exercise. It revolves around identifying all the different cultural contexts for a brand to participate in and all the different audiences to address.

When a brand is present across different cultural contexts, it is nimble and reactive to unexpected cultural moments and can seize them quickly. A sudden wild popularity of Stanley Cup immediately caused a series of media amplifications, leading to a spike in sales to $750 million in 2023 (more than ten times its usual annual revenue).[3] By being present across cultural contexts, brands are able to recognize early cultural conversations, trends and emerging aesthetics and use them to amplify their own cultural products.

Creative media amplification also targets a variety of audiences: not just the brand's current and prospective customers but also cultural creators, commentators, observers, critics and curators. All of these groups have a role in sharing and adoption of cultural products. They are critical for turning cultural products into market hits.

Timelines of influence of different cultural products vary: a piece of content or an ad gets picked up faster and can be amplified quicker than merch or a collaboration.

Even when something becomes a cultural hit, it may take time for it to turn into a market hit. Calvin Klein's video was an instantly successful, with 40 million views on this brand's Instagram and 86% of year-on-year brand engagement increase. During this same period, Calvin Klein's stock fell 20% and sales in North America dropped 8% YoY.[4] Revenue is a lagging indicator of cultural influence, and to close the gap, brands need to keep making cultural products and amplifying them through media.

The idea is to create a self-enforcing loop of different cultural products, each seeded in a different cultural context and targeted at a specific customer segment mostly likely to respond to it. After the wild success of its Jeremy Allen White video, Calvin Klein should have kept at it, quickly releasing merch, figuring out collaborations, additional content entertainment teasers and trailers, in order to keep the cultural influence going. David and Victoria Beckham made the most of their documentary scene, which quickly became a meme, then a T-shirt, and finally and Uber Eats ad over the course of six months – with each of these cultural products amplifying one another.

The first step in the process of implementing hit-making is to figure out the cultural moment and mood, and those setting it. This mood is going to turbocharge a brand's cultural influence and be a fertile ground for its cultural products, increasing their chance of becoming hits. Hit-making is the strategy of cultural influence that defines which cultural products brands should produce to tell their story, whom this story is likely to influence most and in which context, what the most opportune cultural moment is, and what the expected financial returns are.

In this book, readers will learn how to redefine brand marketing as the strategy of cultural influence and how to:

- Develop and convey a brand story.
- Create cultural products and devise media plans to amplify their cultural influence.
- Set up marketing as creative production.
- Build your brand stack so all creative products and brand applications deliver on the brand promise.
- Segment your audience based on their relationship to culture.
- Define and execute the cultural influence strategy.
- Set the organization organizationally and operationally for hit-making.

In this book, readers will find analysis, observations, case studies, interviews, strategy and tactics in the following four chapters.

Chapter 1: importance of the story

"You can have the best technology, you can have the best business model, but if the storytelling isn't amazing, it won't matter. Nobody will watch," noted Jeff Bezos.[5] A clear and compelling brand story ensures that a brand's products and advertising cannot be mistaken for anything else. It gives company context and substance, which helps increase its desirability. When brands sell products, they are selling a story. When consumers buy products, they are buying into this story. A clear brand story internally unifies the organization and streamlines the decision-making. It connects brand editorial with its products, steers design into a narrative and streamlines merchandising, styling and marketing.

Chapter 2: cultural products

A deep dive in the portfolio of cultural products available at the brands disposal to tell their stories. Together, this portfolio builds a creative universe. Some of the cultural products are archives, content, capsules, moments of interest, collaborations, product reboots and sequels, experiences and experiential retail, entertainment, merch, styling and events. Each of these creative executions amplifies and augments one another, and synchronized, they together create a frequency in culture.

Chapter 3: media amplification

Media amplification inserts a brand's cultural products in variety of cultural contexts. In some of these contexts, a brand's cultural products will flourish; in others, they won't get noticed. Media's job is to recognize these contexts – cultural conversations, trends and emerging aesthetics – and use them to amplify a brand's own cultural products. In addition to seasonal campaigns, cultural influence strategy provides snippets of always-on content, merch and products, and creative collaborations that introduce novelty, and to plan its seasonal campaigns as entertainment products, like movies – through teasers, trailers, opening nights and launches. The strategy of cultural influence is a calculated cultural and business test: some executions grow bigger than others, but the job of brand marketing is to synchronize all of them, amplify them through media, and augment them through in-store experiences, content, membership programs, styling and visual merchandising. By connecting all its creative executions, across functions, brands create a self-enforcing loop of cultural influence.

Chapter 4: the creative class

Media amplification targets a variety of audiences: not just a brand's current and prospective customers but also cultural creators, commentators, observers, critics and curators. All of these groups have a role in sharing and adoption of cultural products. They are critical for their potential success, and consequently, for the brand desirability and affinity. These audiences are known as the creative class. They direct wider consumers' attention, time and money toward aspirational things, places and ideas. No consumer makes decisions in isolation from its context – and members of the creative class influence and shape this context through their own consumption.

Notes

1 Frost, S. (2023, December 19). Michael Jordan was fined $5000 for every NBA game due to Nike sponsorship violation. *The Mirror.* https://www.mirror.co.uk/sport/other-sports/american-sports/michael-jordan-nba-nike-fine-30406863

2 John, C. (2024, April 24). Michael Jordan brand can potentially boost $142 billion worth Nike with this annual event. *Essentially Sports.* https://www.essentiallysports.com/nba-legends-basketball-news-michael-jordan-brand-can-potentially-boost-one-hundred-forty-two-billion-worth-nike-with-this-annual-event/

3 Vega, N. (2023, December 23). How a 40-ounce cup turned Stanley into a $750 million a year business. *CNBC.* https://www.cnbc.com/2023/12/23/how-a-40-ounce-cup-turned-stanley-into-a-750-million-a-year-business.html

4 Rockeman, O. (2024, April 1). PVH falls most since 1987 crash on warning of Europe stumble. *Bloomberg.* https://www.bloomberg.com/news/

articles/2024-04-01/calvin-klein-owner-pvh-tumbles-20-on-warning-of-europe-weakness?embedded-checkout=true

5 D'Onfro, J. (2015, July 16). 17 quotes that show how Jeff Bezos turned Amazon into a $200 billion company over 20 years. *Business Insider*. https://www.businessinsider.com/amazon-ceo-jeff-bezos-quotes-2015-7

The importance of storytelling 1

"You can have the best technology, you can have the best business model, but if the storytelling isn't amazing, it won't matter. Nobody will watch," noted Jeff Bezos.[1] A clear and compelling brand story ensures that a brand's products and advertising cannot be mistaken for anything else. It gives a company context and substance, which helps increase its desirability. A clear brand story internally unifies the organization and streamlines the decision-making. It connects the brand editorial with its products, steers design into a narrative and streamlines merchandising, styling and marketing. In addition to being a valuable brand currency, brand storytelling is also critical for customer acquisition and loyalty. Once consumers buy into a brand story, they are less likely to leave or switch than when they just buy a product. Most critically, a good brand story guides which creative products are developed and outlines their rollout and their media amplification strategy.

DOI: 10.4324/9781003534907-2

Without stories, there are no brands

Brand storytelling is going through a renaissance. Pushed aside by performance and influencer marketing, and marred by the declining TV and print formats, brand storytelling was considered something CMOs say at panels when at a loss for alternative.

Stories are all the brands got. A brand itself is a story, invented to give products and services a context and meaning; brands separate products from commodities. When differences in quality or design are minor, a brand sways consumers from one product to another, regardless of price. We pay more to wear something from a certain brand; we use a brand as both identification and differentiation mechanism. Without stories, there are no brands.

Humans are storytelling animals, who tell each other stories to make sense of the world. Pop culture is a story; it provides narrative continuity and cohesion to a lot of sub-stories and micro-narratives. Brands are part of culture. They contribute to its narrative with their own stories. Aside from being corporate and economic entities, brands are also tools that we use to make sense of the world. If we buy Nike, we identify as athletes. If we date on Bumble, we put forward a certain set of values and preferences. If we stay at the Four Seasons, we signal our status and taste. When we wear or use a brand's product or services, we tell a story about ourselves.

Brand stories give consumers a non-economic reason to buy something. It is not transactional (this is why it is harder to directly measure its impact). Brand marketing is cultural, social, psychological and emotional. Brand marketing's purpose is not only to get us to buy something but to buy into something.

In companies across categories, brand storytelling still mostly belongs to the function of brand marketing. The main purpose of brand marketing is to make commodities aspirational, turning their use value into exchange value (social, cultural and environmental capital, which I described in detail in my book *The Business of Aspiration*[2]). There are only so many Loro Piana Open Knitted Walk shoes one can own, but not if they are released in the limited run of 600 for the Gstaad Guy[3] followers.

Through stories, brand marketing gives symbolic value to ordinary consumption.

This symbolic value makes a commodity – a dress or a lipstick or a bottle of green juice – superior to its competition: a very few people will pick Victoria Beckham's T-shirt for $150 over a similar Uniqlo or a GAP one, but many will select "My dad had a Rolls-Royce" one[4] to add some flex to their cultural savvy. Brand marketing transforms non-culture (a T-shirt) into culture (the Beckham's documentary scene and countless memes that it generated). When a person wears a VB shirt, they show off their cultural awareness and also see themselves through a new lens: not as a consumer but as a cultural player.

"Those who can't play, pay!" says MSCHF's $1K limited-edition Ultimate Participation Trophy for Tiffany[5] (Tiffany, among other things, creates sports medals and trophies for US athletes, including US Open). Inside jokes and riffs keep people interested in a brand, and brands that use them enjoy a temporary monopoly over their competition: owner-ship of a subculture is hard to replicate. This goes back to Duchamp and Warhol, who made their way into museums by turning mundane into a work of art by enriching it with pop references and context.

The storytelling stack

Best brand stories create the entire worlds. Beyond traditional media formats, like print and TV, there is an entire toolbox of merch, retail experiences, installations, social media, communities and creators, and content and entertainment that builds worlds. Like Marvel Cinematic Universe, brands need to develop their own narrative universes.

The core premise of a narrative universe is to have a simple and clear vision, mission and promise. Each world is built around one, single idea, which is repeated constantly and consistently. This one idea can generate others, but a world always needs to have an anchor – an archetype or a primary emotion. For Apple, it's creativity. For Disney, it's magic. For Amazon, it's convenience.

Building narrative universes is the preferred brand growth model, and brands increasingly strive to become synonymous with the entire ways of life. In his March 7, 2024, interview with *Financial Times*,[6] Patrizio Bertelli, the former CEO of Prada, a luxury fashion brand, noted that he sees value in "creating an identity that transcends what we sell. We want it to be a mindset, an experience centered around the Prada brand . . . After all, the definition of luxury nowadays is quality of life in every aspect, including what we eat, how we travel, the art and culture we have access to, and what we wear."

In Prada's case, art, design, food and fashion are combined into a recognizable Prada creative universe. In the post-mono culture, retail and media, having a creative universe is a matter of necessity. Brands weave a network of distinct but connected lifestyle verticals, brand experiences and ways to influence culture that, instead of a mass audience, reach a number of taste communities. In this way, they are able to meet niche demands in a segmented, mature fashion retail market, where customers are bored and products are commodified. By catering to its different customer segments, a brand increases its hold on the market and create many doors into the brand.

A narrative universe protects brands from having to "cut through the noise" and forcefully command consumer attention. A narrative world creates a lot of simultaneous signals. Once synchronized – like crickets or lightbulbs – they create a frequency that resonates within culture.

Modern brand stories are vibrations that become strong enough for the culture to hear.

The elements outlined here provide a template for building a brand's narrative universe:

Brand vision outlines the future of the company: where do you see your company in 10 years? What is your North Star? What do you need to do today to get where you want to be in a decade? A brand vision needs to be simple and clear (e.g., Patagonia's brand vision is for our planet to have future). It summarizes a company's aspirations and the impact that it creates, unites employees and directs internal decision-making. A brand vision needs to be aspirational, ambitious and realistic. A clear vision statement is a filter for company's strategic plans (it answers the question of whether a specific strategic direction or a decision drives you towards or away from your vision). It is also a benchmark and a reference point used to review company performance, set KPIs and define company's behavior. (For example, and given its vision, Patagonia became a certified B-corp and its founder gave 98% of the company's proceeds to a charity combating climate crisis[7]).

Brand mission defines what your company does and what business it is in. For example, Banana Republic, a premium fashion brand, is in the business of affordable luxury, so its product quality, pricing, store and website experience and brand communication all convey the positioning of luxury at a great value. Brand mission informs brand positioning and competitive strategy, its business model and growth plan, product assortment strategy, sales targets and marketing budgets. Since Patagonia's vision is for our planet to have the future, the business it is in is creating durable clothes that can be repaired. Brand mission is a springboard for annual business goals and strategy of accomplishing them.

Brand promise is literally what a brand promises to deliver to its customers and fans: it can be intangible benefits, like fun, belonging, status signaling and differentiation, or tangible benefits, like the fastest delivery, lowest price and best quality. It can also be a combination of the two. Brand promise is best when succinctly stated, as it is a filter for all practical business and brand decisions and provides a common goal for all functions in the organization. Brand promise unites product, customer experience, marketing and sales.

A clear brand promise communicates the company's differentiation from its competitors, has a strong position in customers' minds in terms of value that they can expect from the brand, focuses employees as it provides a common decision-making filter, and defines what a brand should be measuring when it comes to its marketing and sales.

This promise needs to reflect a brand's vision and mission, as well to be coveted, desirable and relevant to customers. Best brand promises take the corporate business strategy and marry it with consumer insights.

Brand promise is delivered through brand applications. It provides a template for how to organize and prioritize brand applications and how to connect them into a strategy. It also defines the brand pillars (top emotional attributes of the brand) and brand applications metrics. Brand application metrics define data that captures how well customer interactions with the brand, across touchpoints, align with the brand promise and whether those interactions are aligned with customer expectations.

Brand applications are all the different creative, commercial, experiential and comms ways that a brand promise is delivered to customers. Brand applications are how customers and fans are experiencing a brand, perceiving it, differentiating it from other brands in the market, and also how they engage and relate to it. The most important thing for brand applications is for them to be aligned and consistent, globally and across markets. All brand application come from a single brand promise and a single-mindedly deliver on the brand vision and mission, but are adjusted and flexed through local customer behaviors, market reality, and tech landscape. Brand applications cover the following areas:

a. Product covers product pyramid, including approach to the brand archives (if any), seasonal collections, capsules, and collectible

products. In addition to product strategy, in this category, there is definition of a signature brand look and styling direction, along with
the scope and brand direction or merch used to promote collections,
capsules or collectibles.

b. Retail covers brand communication and sales channels, like website, app, email and physical store experience, including pop-ups
and activations. All these touchpoints need to have a consistent
brand application and very clear and measurable business objectives, including the strategy that connects them all into one consistent
brand experience and one integrated growth plan.

c. Brand communication covers content, social, fandom and cultural
influence. Brand content is a brand's editorial expression of its story
and narrative. This narrative spans across different sales and communication channels, media formats, and has different business purposes
(sales, marketing, brand). Once defined, all these goals and tasks are
integrated into a content strategy and its rollout plan. Social media
have an active role to sell a brand's products and services and the
content strategy applied to social channels needs to be done in sync
with a brand's commercial and communication goals. Fandom is
created and managed through content and social channels, together
with collaborations, partnerships, sponsorships and capsules that
connect and address a specific subculture and/or community. This
is the overlap with cultural influence, which has purpose of defining

a brand's role in culture and its cultural output that goes beyond product sales and covers brand experience, collaborations, influencer and creator management, archive reissues and cultural programming.

d. Creative expression covers creative and art direction for the brand, expressed in the brand experience across retail, social, content and selection of talent. Specific photographers, models, creative directors, props, locations, hair and makeup artists, graphic designers and illustrators all deliver on the brand promise and the creative and art directions that are selected to activate it. Here we also have a brand system, with defined and recognizable brand codes, like monograms, color palette, patterns and prints, font and graphic elements.

The critical part of any narrative universe template – and its successful execution – is to synchronize all brand applications in order to deliver desired business and brand results. For this, all brand applications need to have both clear business and brand objectives, a defined role in the overall business plan, and measurable KPIs. Brand vision, mission and promise remain just statements on paper unless they are produced, tested, and refined through brand applications.

Storytelling primer

The specifics of building a brand's narrative world are threefold: a world-building cheatsheet, which specifies a series of questions to help brands tell their story; a story map, which connects the main theme of the brand story with its sub-narratives aimed at different audience segments and cultural audiences into a narrative universe; and a narrative rollout, which specifies the sequence and the connection between the story elements and connects brand story with its financial returns. The story rollout is considered in regards to the financial investment a brand makes into its narrative, and it has defined KPIs to make it financially accountable.

These three narrative world pillars are detailed as follows:

World-building cheatsheet. Every brand has its own creative universe. The way this universe is experienced by a brands different audiences is a matter of storytelling. Most appropriate narrative format for the modern culture is interstitial storytelling, where there are continuous narrative bursts that are connected into a web of a wider story.

Story map. Define how many sub-narratives does your brand narrative have. The role of sub-narratives is to support the main format of the story, which is usually told through campaign imagery and editorial. These sub-narratives use different formats (e.g., an event, social content, a curation) and create mini-worlds that form the narrative galaxy.

Each of the sub-narratives consists of:

- Social media creative direction and its executions on Instagram, Facebook, TikTok, Pinterest, etc.; storytelling formats (video, collages, carousels, animation, drawings, stop-motion); and art direction for social photography and video.

- Anchor products and product edit.

- Editorial tone of voice and copy.

- Visual merchandising refreshes.

- Merch drops (which merch does a brand want to develop for each sub-narrative?).

- Paid social creative and performance media allocation.

- Influencer and creator selection for each of the sub-narratives.

Narrative rollout. Best brand stories address multiple brand audiences and create many doors into a brand. To this end, a brand story is told as a series of sub-narratives, with each piece of content containing hooks to the next story and ending with a cliffhanger. For retail brands, this means releasing collections like movies, starting with teaser trailers, then trailers, then marketing activations, with the role of building anticipation for a collection release rather than marketing a collection once it is available.

Narrative production

To build narrative worlds, brands need to radically reimagine the way they produce their stories. Aside of Phoebe Philo, a luxury fashion designer, who doesn't believe in brand storytelling (and can afford not to), brand narratives have increasingly been distributed from product design across other areas of business. Marketing, merchandising, cultural influence, collaborations, and PR and events all create the context for the product to be discovered, embraced and propagated and need to be managed accordingly.

Brand narratives are today a matter of organizational design. Product alone cannot win, and neither can just the brand or the business. Bringing them all together is a challenge of creative production.

Consider Gucci: Sabato De Sarno's new designs started trickling into stores only in mid-February of 2024, nearly six months after his first presentation and only two of Gucci's flagships have been transformed into De Sarno's new brand narrative. Gucci's Q1 results[8] are not the failure of design; they are a failure of production.

Just like an entertainment company pulls in the different talent to deliver a movie or a television show, brands need to do the same – to produce not just their seasonal collections but their entire creative and business narrative.

Pharrell Williams is an exceptional producer who understands entertainment and the need for ongoing content, events and drops. His Louis Vuitton work doesn't only adhere to the fashion calendar but also creates moments in-between, like store openings, launches, new product drops, and exclusive capsules (most recently with Tyler, the Creator[9]).

For Jacquemus, a fashion brand, narrative production unifies fun products (double-heeled strappy sandals), fun bits of content (Instagram), fun art direction, fun retail experience and fun stunts. Casablanca, another fashion brand, similarly produces an upbeat and joyful world, where brand products are part of the experience and a lifestyle.

More than narrative production, these examples point to the business transformation.

Traditional business models revolve around sourcing, production, distribution, and sales and marketing of products and services. With the increasing number of brands and consumer choice overload, the pressure for newness and innovation, and increasing number of sales and marketing channels, this model has been stretched to its limits. So far, the solution has been to make this model more efficient, and marketing more spectacular and expensive, with diminishing returns. This winners-take-all scenario makes the already big brands bigger, at the expense of smaller, emerging and new brands. (An often-quoted example of this kind of obliviousness is Kodak, which kept making the process of manufacturing and distributing chemical-based film more efficient, instead of figuring out how to adapt to digital photography. Blockbuster is another example, and the entire media industry is yet another.)

Instead of making the current business models more efficient, better is to spread the pressure for innovation, novelty, and profit from creative departments to everyone else. When creative departments are not given enough time to develop constant innovation, then making the innovation process more distributed among functions can help.

Instead of a single product or service, innovation in fashion is now a matter of producing a creative stack. Just like entertainment companies produce an entertainment stack around their creative output (including marketing, distribution, events, PR, activations, merch, etc.), brands creative stack consists of the product and the innovative ways of bringing it to market.

Marketing, distribution, merchandising, retail experience, merch and PR are not anymore separate from products and services; they are part of the same stack, and custom-made for each. This requires creative collectives in place of siloed organizations, lateral collaboration instead of top-down management, and distributed instead of centralized creativity. Outside of corporations, MSCHF is an example of this kind of creative organization; the frequency and originality of their output has so far been impressive. Their releases are organized like a creative stack: the product is combined with its marketing, distribution and sales.

No single individual can come up with the completely, original, imaginative ideas every season, consistently, for years. But a whole group of people might.

Being innovative in sourcing, production, distribution, merchandising, communication, PR, retail design and experience, social media, community building and fandom management requires a radical rethinking of the business talent and its organization, and a redefinition of the corporate functions and processes. The industries, across categories, have a set of new challenges to address, and they require the same innovative, creative, passionate and curious way it takes to design packaging or come up with a new sparkling water.

A brand-centric organization

To set up their companies to consistently deliver on their brand narrative, brands first need to bridge the gap in their short-term versus long-term thinking. Short-term thinking is marked by expectation of the quick sales results; when they are missing, brand marketing gets cut, driving a company deeper into discount-dependency and increasingly expensive retargeting and other traffic-driving bottom of the funnel tactics. Long-term thinking prioritizes the full-funnel, maintains strategic vs. tactical view, gives time for brand desirability to solidify, and deeply embeds the brand strategy and management across different departments and functions. The challenge is bridging the two.

This bridge is a matter of organizational design. Too often, organizational holistic thinking is missing, and brand is delegated to the domain of marketing (worse yet, just brand marketing), where it is equated with seasonal campaigns, PR and media planning.

Brand storytelling is deeply embedded in product design and merchandising, digital and physical retail, and media and cultural influence. This may sound like an overreach of Napoleonic proportions, but modern organizations have no choice in breaking the silos down and adopting a brand-centric model. There are a lot of brands around, a lot of retail channels and technologies, and a lot of ways to buy something; in this context, only by having a strong brand vision, positioning and aesthetics a brand can successfully compete.

How successful the vision, positioning and aesthetics is translated into a brand's cultural influence and sales is a matter of organizational cooperation. Processes become more important than structure; the structure is flattened; success is a matter of nimble project management and production as much as of the compelling vision and growth strategy.

Brand management is today a strategy of cultural awareness and amplification, an experimental, portfolio approach to brand actions, creation of moments of interest, entertainment production, fandom-building and market expansion.

Brand management synchronizes all brand actions – from email copy to visual merchandising to design concepts and customer relationship management – across departments and functions. By doing this, it protects a brand's pricing power, makes a distinction between margin-drivers and volume-drivers when it comes to products, and constantly renews consumers' brand perception, making the brand relevant.

Brand x product. Brand narrative impacts product design through product pyramid, signature products, the brand look and brand codes. Further, it defines the annual design concepts, in sync with the annual brand theme and its rollout. Brand narrative further manages archives and archival revivals, vintage curation, capsules and special editions, and collaborations and builds narratives around hero products. Finally, brand narrative provides styling guides and brand personas.

Brand x merchandising. Brand narrative influences merchandising through implementation of brand narratives on retail floors. It contextualizes hero products with stories and seasonal collections with lookbooks and styling guides. It puts brand personas front and center, making sure that the product assortment appeals to target customer groups. Brand narrative influences collection rollouts and timing of the drops, and it defines merch to accompany collections.

Brand x retail. In both digital and physical retail, brand narrative is in charge of the product presentation and the tone of voice that brand addresses customers in. Visual handwriting is present through window displays but also through the color palette, styling, product assortment selection, sales and promotional panels design, and selection of the seasonal campaign imagery. Brand and seasonal lookbooks and styling guides educate both customers and sales associates about the brand look. Websites and stores are synchronized through brand in their visual and user experience design, consistent and recognizable as belonging to a single brand. In physical retail, brand designs pop-ups and events, and on the website, it is in charge of art direction for e-commerce, email copy and CRM programs design and copy.

Brand x media. Brand narrative is present throughout the funnel through content, tone of voice, community and membership programs, events, social media, personalization and specialized retail services. By giving brand story priority, media buying and planning focuses on long-term gains in awareness, interest, consideration, advocacy and loyalty, and not just on short-term sales goals. This approach allows a company to protect its brand equity, pricing power and customer base. The focus of media planning are bottoms-up actions that amplify organic brand content distributed through a brand's own channels. In the brand-centric organizations, media is focused on producing, distributing and monetizing a brand's IP.

Brand x cultural influence. In this book, brand management is expanded and redefined as the strategy of cultural influence. Through their strategy of cultural influence, brands define their stories and convey them via cultural products that are amplified through media. In the next chapter, I will explore the categories of cultural products and the creative production behind them.

Notes

1   D'Onfro, J. (2015, July 16). 17 quotes that show how Jeff Bezos turned Amazon into a $200 billion company over 20 years. *Business Insider*. https://www.businessinsider.com/amazon-ceo-jeff-bezos-quotes-2015-7

2 Andjelic, A. (2021). *The business of aspiration: How social, cultural, and environmental capital changes brands.* Routledge.

3 https://www.instagram.com/gstaadguy/reel/CXRYG7kqAY3/

4 https://us.victoriabeckham.com/products/slogan-tee-my-dad-drives-a-rolls-royce-in-white-19451?variant=40693694365738&currency=USD&gad_source=1&gclid=Cj0KCQjwmt24BhDPARIsAJFYKk1pnEgc4YuZ5SQzcMkcrIenvq1rBQtrArID3Ni4RN6eo5xzUn9FRE8aAlfeEALw_wcB&gclsrc=aw.ds

5 https://ultimateparticipationtrophy.com/

6 Borrelli, S. S. (2024, March 7). Prada's Patrizio Bertelli on plans for €1bn retail investment. *Financial Times.* https://www.ft.com/content/ccb5a32d-be04-45f3-92f5-2b8ffaa0a45b

7 https://www.patagonia.com/ownership/

8 Kerin Press Release. (2024, April 23). *First quarter 2024 revenue.* https://www.kering.com/api/download-file/?path=Kering_Press_release_First_quarter_2024_revenue_0cdd2e8116.pdf

9 Leitch, L. (2024, March 21). "I still can't believe this" – Tyler, the creator premieres his capsule for Pharrell Williams and Louis Vuitton. *Vogue.* https://www.lvmh.com/news-documents/news/louis-vuitton-and-pharrell-williams-tap-tyler-the-creator-for-spring-2024-mens-capsule-collection/

Cultural products   **2**

To deliver their cultural influence strategy, brands create cultural products. Then they use cultural products to tell their stories. There are ten categories of cultural products: merch, collaborations, archive reissues, product icons, aesthetics, styling, brand codes, graphic design, retail experiences and entertainment.

The role of cultural products is to renew brand associations, refresh the brand identity, test new ideas in the market and/or test new markets, reinforce the brand positioning, maintain the brand narrative fresh, reinterpret the brand in the ever-evolving culture, and keep the brand dialogue with subcultures, niches, and communities going. Ultimately, cultural products influence consumer decisions-making. Consumers never make decisions in isolation from each other, their social media accounts, streets they walk in, content they watch/listen/read, and images, products, and people they are surrounded by.

DOI: 10.4324/9781003534907-3

Nine categories of cultural products create the brand's narrative universe. Each creative product category refers to, amplifies and augments all others, creating a cultural frequency for the brand. Narrative universe and cultural products are interdependent: cultural products enrich and add halo to the brand story, and brand story connects separate cultural products with its main products and services and into one coherent narrative.

Merch

Is Millionaire Speedy a luxury bag or merch? What about the Balenciaga Maxi Pack?[1] Some people's idea of merch is Trump's gold high-tops. Merch as a status symbol. Merch as a subgenre. Merch as a style statement. Merch as an identity marker. Merch as something of waning cultural relevance.

How old-fashioned

Rather than being a retail's side gig, modern merch has become its main act. Merch has always been a high-margin moneymaker, so a subtle but all-encompassing transformation of retail's operating principle into merch makes economic sense. Through the process of transubstantiation from a youth culture artifact to a killer business model, merch has been turned from its original purpose, meaning and aesthetics into retail's main product category and the only remaining genre. Consumers have learned to buy everything as merch, and there is no going back.

The term "merch" originally referred to items made for music fans, where items like T-shirts were sold on a band's or musician's tour. From music, merch spread to sports, film, gaming, art, fashion, design, travel and entertainment. Merch is often released in special "drops," the unexpected and seemingly random instances when merch becomes available in limited quantities. Information about merch drops is not public and is carefully guarded and traded by those in the know. Knowing what a brand's next drop will be and when it will be released is valuable currency, and source of status in the community, subculture or a taste niche for those who have it.

Merch's value is not in the physical item itself but in the social and cultural capital associated with it. Erewhon, an upscale Los Angeles supermarket, taps with its clothing capsules and collaborations into LA's obsessive health culture and Erewhon as its hub and epicenter, where celebrities meet organic smoothies, which meet aspirational lifestyle, which meets branded clothes. All of these are status symbols in equal measure. Merch's social and cultural capital makes it the opposite of a commodity. Commodities are interchangeable; merch is a unique expression of a specific time, place, community and context. At the height of its fame, a streetwear brand Supreme traced a social and cultural topography of its brand's global community. Through its merch, Supreme held this community together across time and geography. It connected people, conversations and symbols into one Supreme social network. Today, a menswear fashion brand Aimé Leon Dore's Lower East Side community is gathered around its store and also its ideas, aesthetics, references and products. Unlike French sociologist Emile Durkheim's idea of solidarity created by ritual and symbols, ADL's community socializes through merch.

Perhaps the most extreme case of merch socialization is MSCHF's Key4All activation,[2] where one thousand keys that all unlock the same car were released for sale. MSCFH described the idea as the shift from universal basic car to public universal car, where "the entirety of ZipCar was rebuilt with a fleet of one single vehicle." The car, Chrysler PT Cruiser, traveled across the country, connected all the keychain owners into a community, and served as a canvas for their creative expression. MSCHF describes the car as "transient and un-ownable, a journey and temporary blessing," hinting at the interpretative openness of social objects: they are there to be interacted with, commented on, transformed, and interpreted. As one of the keychain owners noted, "the amount of fun we were able to have with this car created a lifetime worth of memories."

Merch is always a physical object and a symbol. "The Ultimate Participation Trophy" by Tiffany & Co. and MSCHF is handcrafted and released in a limited series of 100 trophies.[3] The trophy's physical features combine silver and this brand signature blue color, along with equestrian themes (nodding to the Woodlawn Vase, the first trophy designed by Tiffany & Co.). The trophy's cultural and symbolic capital is twofold. First, it celebrates Tiffany & Co.'s tradition of trophy designs and marks 160th anniversary of Tiffany & Co.'s handcrafting sports trophies at its Rhode Island workshop. Second, it has been made by MSCHF, which endows it with playful, subversive connotations (the figure is riding a horse while holding a ball and swinging a tennis racquet) and speaks to communities and subcultures who are familiar MSCHF and who regard it in the context of this familiarity.

Full readability of "The Ultimate Participation Trophy" requires previous knowledge of MSCHF's work. Like text, merch is more of a process and projection rather than a finished, definitive thing. Tiffany & Co.'s Cat Street Tokyo drop doesn't translate if we are not familiar with Tiffany & Co.'s previous drops and with Cat Street and its social and cultural meaning. Outside of it, Tiffany & Co.'s Cat Street Tokyo merch has little value. Within it, it advances Tiffany & Co.'s brand story and cultural influence. Knowledge of what the new thing is going to be dropped, when, who made it, what came before, and why it is relevant are all layers of social and cultural value that turn a piece of merch into a social and cultural object.

Sometimes, merch turns into a myth object. Nike Air Jordan 1 OG High Chicago are from 1985 and designed by Peter Moore, and today are one of the most iconic and expensive examples of merch. Status-signaling luxury items today also act as merch, as they carry connotations of social and economic standing; high-margin items that luxury brands produce, like keychains, scarves or lipsticks are merch, as they act as signifiers of social class and give their owners association with social and economic status. Anything can be turned into merch if infused with enough symbolic value and cultural capital. There are several types of merch circulating in the cultural markets:

Toys. Toy merch are social objects meant to connect fans and invite play, and are infinitely meme-fiable. They signal that their owners can have whatever they want, but that the traditional fashion aesthetics bores them. Examples are JW Anderson canary and pigeon bags, Thom Browne dog bag, Hermès Quelle Idole bag and Marni green furry pom-pom earrings.

Puns. Wearable puns feature objects at odds with their context or meaning. Examples are Gucci x Balenciaga's the Hacker Project, Balenciaga's IKEA tote bag, Moschino's dresses as pieces of furniture, Off-White, Hermès, Palace's Jesus Gilet and tabloid jacket, JW Anderson asparagus purse, or Bonnie Cashin and Cinzia Ruggieri's glove bag.

Simulation. In a simulation game, real world activities, such as city strolling, sports, or grocery shopping are explored through products: what would you wear if . . . Examples are Erewhon, which turned grocery shopping into a luxury experience; Hermès Bolide bag, which takes its cues from the world of skating, with a base that reflects the shape of a skateboard, decorated with street art; and the Chanel rare collector's runway supermarket grocery basket chain tote minaudière. Other examples are Thom Browne's Fall 2022 inspiration the Island of Misfit Toys.

Fantasy. Fantasy is a game of exploration where players assume the role of a protagonist in a narrative. Fantasy games often have challenges based on puzzles, strategy or action sequences. Examples are oversized sleeves, square shapes, medieval motifs and surrealist interpretations, as in Balenciaga's F/W '21 collection, and surrealist interpretations as can be seen in JW Anderson and Schiaparelli.

Winks. Winks work when details are randomized and represent game elements, such as colors, prints, ideas and moments. Winks are strategic, with every detail having a unique power and message within the game. Examples are Chanel's camellia, damouflage, Hans Kjøbenhavn's "Grip Dress," LL Bean tags, JW Anderson shoes and wearable technology details, McQueen's clutch and Hermès horseshoe bag.

Kitsch. Kitsch is a game that's calculated to provoke through sentimentality and purposeful poor taste meant to be appreciated in an ironic way. Favorite is Casablanca, a fashion brand.

Merch's social and cultural capital makes them collectible. Merch turns brands into collections and consumers into collectors.

A collection is a story that drives products' desirability beyond their commercial value. "The taste for collection is a kind of passionate game,"[4] noted French art auctioneer and historian Maurice Rheims. Symbolic value of items in a collection is amplified through their associations with stories, histories, brands and personalities. A pair of Adidas that belong to Pharrell's collection are more valuable than the same pair sold by an anonymous seller on Grailed. Pharrell's sneaker collection reflects Pharrell's taste, creative identity and curatorial sensibility, and this gives all the items in this collection an aura and halo of Pharrell's cultural influence.

Through cultural associations, collections accumulate social and economic capital that is used by collectors to convey their status and taste. Supreme is a collection of pretty much anything, from a T-shirt to a branded brick to a Tiffany & Co. heart bracelet, held together by Supreme's urban aesthetic shaped by the tight-knit community of skaters and DJs and hypebeasts.

Supreme's narrative links its merch to culture, removes them from their initial use and converts them into parts of a collection. This collection is self-perpetuating: Supreme various collaborations exert externalities on one another and on the Supreme universe. Once it's part of the collection, a Supreme item accrues capital in context of its secondary market value. Media, cultural commentators, communities, collectors, critics, dealers and resellers, and global brands all contribute to the Supreme narrative that amplifies its streetwear origins and participate in the definition of its market value.

Our digital wallets and our social media accounts make us all collectors, and it turns our collections into capital traded in social, cultural and economic currency. The value of the Bored Ape Yacht Club NFT collection is greater because the design of its items is randomized. A rare item with a singular aesthetic, like a Bored Ape with gold fur, appreciates the entire collection. New airdrops also ensure that each collection is profitable, by constantly creating new differences and constant novelty: there's an original 10K drop, there's a mutant serum that transforms original Bored Apes, there's a new mutant drop, and so on. Thanks to their proof of ownership and their secondary royalties, NFTs power-charge the collector economy. NFTs also promise their collectors the future: if you acquire a Bored Ape, for example, you are part of something that's happening and also something that's about to happen.

Collections are increasingly relevant in how consumers assign value to things and in how brands manage demand for goods, services and experiences. Being a collector – and/or assembling a collection – requires active learning to appreciate things and to transition from commercial thinking to cultural thinking.

Collections have no objective intrinsic value. The value of a collection is defined by the community of collectors and their willingness to pay for it. Social demand, based on the perception that a collection is valuable, defines its salability. In contrast to the traditional economy, the collector economy recognizes that taste is socially created and that a community creates consensus on the value, rarity and desirability of a collection.

There are two ways for collections to increase their value:

- Absolute and relative rarity (the number of items in a set, and the number of the same items within a set).
- Strength of a collection's association to a story, aesthetics, identity and values (e.g., Hermès aesthetic mix of equestrianism, playfulness and leisure references).

Liquid Death

Their VP of Creative, Andy Pearson, has described Liquid Death as "really just an amalgamation of all the things that we find interesting –

heavy music, satire, art, absurdist humor, health and environmental issues, sketch comedy – all thrown in a bag and shaken up."[5] The company doesn't believe in pre-testing but practices active, engaged listening, using data from each release to inform the next thing. Since you never know what will succeed, it's a smart strategy. If something doesn't work, that's OK since they're so prolific and never precious.

In addition to the rarity and strength of the narrative, the collection's value is in how the items within it are organized: in its organizing principle. Hermès connects all Birkins into a club – a creative world in which collectors immerse themselves. A Birkin is a passport to enter this world.

Some of the organizing principles of collections are as follows:

Thematic collection. Items in the collection (products, experiences) are connected into a narrative and held together by a specific story. Donna Karan's Seven Easy Pieces, Anine Bing's Classics, "Core by COS" and Zara Origins are some examples. More creative examples include brand history and heritage, like Kanye's Wyoming ranch and Ralph Lauren's American Dream, and also stories around human creativity and ingenuity, like Hermès does in its annual brand themes. In this scenario, a brand's artistic directors and creative directors become curators, which is something that we will be seeing more of: it is not enough for an artistic director to have their design vision. The strength of a brand is how good an artistic director is in using their vision as a curatorial filter in assembling a cultural collection, with their own designs being just one part of it (Alessandro Michele at GUCCI is doing a version of this, with his coherent aesthetic world and narrative-driven collections).

Temporal collection. In this type of collection, items are released serially, and the set is meant to be completed over a period of time. This type of collection is a fertile ground for streetwear brands and "full look" fashion and luxury brands as well as experiences, where each item and experience pre-conditions release of subsequent ones. Completing a collection increases its value and the value of individual objects. The temporal collection model evolves the idea of the drop and turns it into a continuous drip of items needed to complete a collection.

Personal collection. Here, individual taste, creativity and curatorial savvy play a critical role. The most relevant thing with personal collections is for them to be intentional (e.g., items in my closet are not a fashion collection; they are a pile). But learning about, appreciating and amassing vintage Celine becomes a personal collection.

Community collection. This type of collection will be more prominent with the evolution of DAOs, where members of a DAO invest in acquiring objects for a collection and collectively own this collection themselves. DAO-based collecting simultaneously creates economic, social and cultural value and creates a new class of owners and a new social class of investors and collectors. A recent attempt of a DAO to buy a copy of the

US Constitution is an example and is applicable to collecting anything from art to fashion to fine wines to real estate and beyond.

Collections have their own market logic, competitive dynamics and growth models. In aspirational economy, where it is imperative for products to be differentiated, original, personalized, and connected by storytelling, merch and collections are the mechanism for increasing brand value and opportunities for brand growth. With aesthetization of our everyday life, products and experiences, we seek need to be meaningful, beautiful, artful and story-rich. They also need to be constantly reinvented and refreshed. Collections simultaneously ensure singularity, connectivity and continuity of merch they organize.

On the brand level, collections work by creating an aesthetic and ethic universe in which experiences, products, stories and communities mutually enrich one another. Within this brand universe, collections are potentially infinite, as long as every new collection is linked to the brand history or story, starting with its name. The theme and the name of a collection should be meaningful within a brand universe and should echo a brand's core experience promise. Each new collection has its own story that fits into the wider brand story and that renews it and furthers it.

On the product design level, developing a collection becomes a conceptual and creative exercise that focuses on creating a story and a setting that the collections' items convey. Design elements like silhouette, color palette and other details semantically link items together and make them different from other collections in the same brand (and from all other brands). Collections here emphasize one-offs and uniqueness of an item and randomization of its properties (color, elements of the brand system like logos and monograms). Curation becomes a critical part of the product design process, where each design decision is taken through the curatorial lens of the particular collection.

Collaborations

Rimowa's collaboration with espresso machine maker La Marzocco seems like something out of MSCHF, an art collective. Known for its purposefully absurd and seemingly random stunts, which regularly become cultural hits, MSCHF broke into the scene with Nike sneakers filled with holy water, cartoon-like Big Red Boots, and the Global Supply Chain Telephone Handbag, among other hits. However, it certainly wouldn't look out of place next to the MSCHF's Catchup or Makeup, a limited-edition exclusive Linea Mini debuted on April 15, 2024, during Milan Design Week, in two pop-up stores/cafes, set by Rimowa and by La Marzocco.

Collaborations like Travis Scott and McDonald's, Simone Rocha and Crocs, Fendi and FRGMT and Pokémon, and Tag Heuer and Formula One and Kith are often dismissed as stunt-y, tongue-in-cheek, garish and lowbrow. Be that as it may, most of them aim to be appreciated in an ironic and knowing way.

Good collaborations are art; great collaborations are kitsch.

Great collaborations fit into the definition of kitsch perfectly: a replica that's purposefully fake, and that's where the joke is. Take it seriously, and you are a goon.

There are already obvious parallels between collaborations and the world of art (and kitsch): there are auctions, collectors, dealers, critics, resale marketplaces and monographs. Just like art, collaborations aim to shock and surprise. They can't be criticized, and they strive to reach high prices and cultural immortality.

"You know it's art when the check clears," said Andy Warhol. With Roy Lichtenstein and Robert Indiana, Warhol made his way into museums by turning the mundane world into works of art by enriching it with pop references, connotations and associations. Warhol's art is commercial and his commercials are art (a Warhol ad launched Absolut vodka in 1986).

At the same time, fine art went from museums into fashion, design and pop culture. Elsa Schiaparelli – the original creator of the newspaper print dress – was probably the proto fashion collaborator who featured her surrealist friends like Salvador Dali on her designs. In the '80s, New York designer Willi Smith invited artists, performers and graphic designers to join his project of making art part of daily life. In the early '00s, Jeff Koons, Damien Hirst, Takashi Murakami and Stephen Spouse joined forces with Louis Vuitton where then creative director Marc Jacobs turned the fashion-art collaboration into global cash cows. Recently, Cindy Sherman collaborated with Undercover and Yayoi Kusama has just released her new Veuve Clicquot La Grande Dame limited-edition bottle and gift box. It retails for $30,000 and comes with a poem.

When someone buys a Cindy Sherman x Undercover, they aren't actually buying a bag or a T-shirt; they're buying a legit work of art. When they wear it, a person shows off their knowledge and cultural awareness. They also see themselves through a new lens: not as mere consumers but as collectors. Done right, collaborations generate collectibles, justify high prices, create cult objects, and initiate brands in the domain of intangibles. Thanks to this newly acquired timelessness, symbolic authority and post-materialistic form, Undercover isn't a mere commercial entity but a shrine of culture and human creativity. Through collaborations, brands ingrain themselves in culture, not in a market segment.

Like other cultural products, collaborations transform non-culture into culture. It's a great business model: collaborations don't need financial capital, only a strong brand capital. Supreme can put its logo on a brick and collaborate with Colgate as long as its brand equity is attractive.

Moncler, Mini and Aim Leon Dore made collaborations integral parts of their DNA, and with good reason: compressed trend cycles force brands to constantly come up with the new stuff. Consumers today expect physical products at the unattainable speed of Instagram. A quick solve is to riff off already popular and familiar stuff. Cue in the endless Air Jordan and Supreme collaborations. A brand uses Air Jordan or Supreme's aesthetic just enough to become kitsch, which gives it a new context and an ironic read and turns it into an insider joke.

Collaborations work well in mature markets, where consumers are bored and products are commodified. There are only so many Uniqlo items that a person can own, but not if those items were made by Jun Takashi, Jil Sander or Pharrell. Having the fashion link allows Uniqlo to cultivate "elitism to all": it can sell a lot of Pharrell T-shirts to a lot of people without diluting its symbolic value. This symbolic value makes a commodity incomparable: a very few people will pick Rimowa La Marzocco over Nespresso or Breville in a store. But many will select it to add some flex to their kitchens. Limited editions keep the cultural pioneers interested in the brand, and La Marzocco can enjoy a temporary monopoly by rendering its competition irrelevant: collaborations are hard to replicate.

Hardest to replicate are inconsistent and random collaborations, like Travis Scott and McDonald's or Fendi and Pokémon. Their genius is in that they shun any coherence. Coherence is for suckers, because collaborations aren't brand extensions. They're a creative expression of a brand that let it flex its cultural muscles, promote it as a trendsetter and turn its products into brand communication. A Chanel snowboard or IKEA x Craig Green make Chanel and IKEA modern and culturally present and curious.[6] An unexpected collaboration attracts collectors, cultural pioneers and hypebeasts. It becomes the source of a brand's cultural influence.

For a brand, having repeated cultural hits is everything. In the modern economy, the growth motor isn't a price. It's taste, aesthetics, identity and thrill. Economic growth comes not from products but from the cultural influence that a brand creates. Products are just a vehicle for beauty, thrill, identity, transformational experiences and a life aesthetically worth living. Rimowa luggage, in its own words, is on a mission to create essential tools for a lifetime of travel. By collaborating with La Marzocco, Rimowa put this mission on steroids. It makes Rimowa luggage more present in its customers' lives and more personally relevant. Having a luggage-maker coffee machine turns the everyday into an adventure. Every time we make coffee in Linea Mini, we create a social distance between ourselves as those unenlightened enough to use Nespresso. We also create a link between us and all other cultural pioneers.

Collaborations aren't a brand gloss. They're a strategic transformation of a brand's cultural influence strategy. In the aspirational economy, this transformation is a matter of a brand's long-term renewal and relevance. Strategic collaborations across a brand's entire value chain are akin to making a safe bet on a brand's cultural and business future.

At the level of marketing and sales, collaborations protect pricing power, ensure high margins and reframe consumers' perception of the brand. At the level of a product concept and production, collaborators provide value innovation. At the level of distribution, collaborations expand a brand's market and renew its customer base. A collaboration between luxury brands and Chinese KOLs give these brands an in with the Chinese customer. A collaboration between Louis Vuitton and cultural pioneers like Travis Scott renews brand associations. At the level of merchandising, collaborations give halo to the core collection, re-evaluate brand perception and increase brand consideration. Before Nike launches a new model, it seeds it on runways of its fashion collaborators like Undercover or Sacai. The collaborators add their imprint, making it culturally noteworthy and spurring interest in the model's later commercial release by Nike.

Collaborations are basically a constant brand recontextualization: they take it from one context and put it into another one. In that sense, there isn't "bad" collaboration: collaborations are calculated cultural and business tests. Some contexts are more fertile than others, but just as evolution constantly mixes stuff up to see what sticks (theropods didn't), a brand stays alive through remixes. Collaborations are the strategy of brand awareness, market expansion and its fountain of youth.

Through recontextualization, collaborations:

- [a]llow brands to start trading in exchange value, not in use value. Use value is defined by a product's functionality. Exchange value is defined by a product's social appeal. A cultural hit becomes a market hit. Brands that insert their products in the cultural exchange system and not just in a market segment, win.

- Give everyday products identity. In a crowded competitive landscape, a brand is the key product differentiator. A brand makes products stand for something more than their function and separates them from commodities. A collaboration enforces brand identity, ensures its continuity and connects products into a narrative.

- Infuse taste and meaning into ordinary consumption. Today, a brand's products and services do not only fulfill their basic functions. Their job is to aesthetically enrich their buyers' lives and become social links that signal status, social distinction and belonging.

Collaborations are easier to understand once they're taken out the domain of brand stunts and into the domain of culture. Culture is a big business. Culture is also a big social and cultural commentator, critic and cynic. It tells us what we need to know about the world we live in and about where the future is going. Collaborations do the same.

To approach collaborations strategically, refer to the following framework as an example. Brands selected for collaborations need to fulfill at one of the following goals (or a combination):

a. Amplify your brand's assortment.

b. Complement your brand's assortment.

c. Diversify your brand's assortment.

Amplify

In this category are brands that amplify your brand's positioning, product offering and cultural resonance. The best recent brand amplification collaborations are Swarovski x Skims, Mango x Boglioli, Steven Meisel x Zara, Matches x Missoni, Rabanne x H&M, Telfar x UGGs, and Omega x Swatch.

Complement

In this category are brands that complement your brand's seasonal and category product offerings. A capsule, a drop, a merch or a special collection isn't something that your brand regularly offers, and this type of collaboration serves to renew your brand's audience proposition. Examples are Rimowa x Tiffany & Co., Nike x Tiffany & Co., Birkenstock x Tekla, Miu Miu x New Balance, and Bode x Nike.

Diversify

In this category are brands that take your brand into new categories and retail territories. This is the domain of non-sequiturs, cultural stunts, randomness, kitsch and experimentation. Examples are Rimowa x Tiffany & Co., Nike x Tiffany & Co., Birkenstock x Tekla, Miu Miu x New Balance, anything that MSCHF does, Typo x Barbie, Christian Cowan x Teletubbies, Nike x Ben & Jerry's, Pokémon x Van Gogh, Fenty Beauty x MSCHF.

Best brand partners display:

a. Brand alignment with your brand: they have a similar ethos.

b. Product alignment: an aesthetic connection.

c. Cultural alignment: they make your brand relevant and current.

Within this strategic decision-making framework, choose one or both of the following approaches for your brand collaboration:

a. Choose a partner that will creatively reinterpret your signature products, either through their own internal team or through external creators, artists, designers, curators, stylists, etc. Example: Tiffany & Co.

b. License your brand signifiers (logo, brand codes, color palette, signature prints) to other brands. Example: Supreme.

The final part of collaborations strategy is to make it part of the production, distribution, marketing and sales rollout plan. Build a production and distribution timeline. Connect it with your entire product line and marketing activations. Think holistically and in terms of a halo effect that a collaboration will have on your entire brand. Tie a collaboration to a collection and campaign rollout, and use it to build interest in your own's brand products. Release a collaboration beforehand to garner PR and press and then bring it home through your own collection.

Archive reissues

On the most basic, functional level, a Chanel 22 handbag is made for carrying things and is priced based on its performance and features like materials and labor. The handbag's value equals its performance and price.

But if we were to know the unique story and heritage of Chanel and how this handbag embodies it, a new valuation logic opens up. Made known, material history gets to dictate a product's value: Chanel handbags are adorned with Coco Chanel's famous initials and associated with luxury for every single person in the world. They are reminders of talent and inventiveness of Chanel's designs, of sophistication and chicness of Paris, and of Chanel's dialogue with culture through its iconic brand codes, advertising, stores and the founder's famous suite in the Ritz. These brand origins make Chanel 22 handbag a Trojan horse of culture: of the context, collective and individual intention, and social impetus that inspired them.

Past is valuable because it differentiates a brand from everyone else. Even a brand that doesn't have any real past or heritage can invent it. Ralph Lauren empire is built on an invented story of the American East Coast aristocracy. Louis Vuitton's story has been enriched and expanded and turned into a heritage. A brand heritage comes from founders but also from neighborhoods and provenances. "Made in France" is linked to the story of French cultural activity and heritage. "Made in Detroit" was similarly linked to Shinola, a bicycle brand, heritage until it turned to be at least partially fake. Attaching a new or the existing brand to the past differentiates its products from commodities (a commodity like a Shein T-shirt doesn't have a story).

The true innovation here is in reactivating the past in a way that is simultaneously surprising and familiar or, as Raymond Loewy, the father of industrial design, noted: "to sell something surprising, make it familiar; and to sell something familiar, make it surprising."[7] Balenciaga products live in many interpretations, depending on who the collaborator is. Brands like Chrome Hearts, Off-White, Heron Preston or A-Cold-Wall* all make their mark by combining the recognizable with the slightly different. Like jazz or streetwear, they put forward a repetition in many forms.

Making the familiar feel new through fresh connections to culture can indeed revitalize struggling brands, but the fastest way back to cultural relevance is still to deconstruct what made a brand successful in the first place.

Brand archives are a goldmine of beloved, and often forgotten, brand classics. As a brand grows and matures, it often forgets the spark that started it all. But the old favorites that are part of the brand lore have the power to quickly re-engage both legacy and new fans by tapping into their real or invented nostalgia.

The Banana Republic rebranding started in June 2021 with its first ever vintage store, on Fifth Avenue in New York and online.[8] We partnered with Thrilling, a vintage sourcing and authentication vendor, on a number of curated vintage Banana Republic items, ranging from T-shirts and sweaters to leather vests and jackets. The vintage capsule launch was used to remind customers about storied Banana Republic archives and the role that this iconic brand once had in culture. It was also a vehicle of reaching out to younger consumers through 1980s and 1990s nostalgia, original brand aesthetics, and secondhand clothes.

At Milan Design Week 2024, Stone Island revealed the latest edition of its "Prototype Research" project.[9] "Prototype Research" is a limited-edition series that is currently in its eighth iteration. The premise of the series to play with fabric innovation that is in the core of Stone Island's DNA. Part creative lab, part research facility, part design studio, "Prototype Research" aims to refresh the brand identity through showcasing material innovation techniques that are not yet scaled up to be used in annual collections. Inspiration behind each of the editions are the first Stone Island collections from the early 1980s, and Stone Island notes that "returning to the archive allows the team to instill foundational garments with 'new ideas and evolved technologies.'"

In 2022, the Gucci 100 centennial campaign paid tribute to the brand's history and impact on pop culture. It featured an exclusive collection of items that harken back to the brand's century of fashion. Gucci launched 100 pop-up stores, as well as Spotify and Apple playlists featuring music that paid homage to the company's enduring aesthetic. By evoking the brand's themes through music, while mixing it with Gucci's new and archival products, Gucci traded on its heritage and extended its product lifecycles.

This strategy can help to transport a brand's history into the present and remind people of the product innovations that made the brand great in the first place. But it's not enough to simply remix old products. Brands must transport that heritage to new customers and modern values. Gucci recently launched Vault, a site where the brand mixes old favorites with new designers who emphasize Gucci brand values, such as diversity, gender neutrality and sustainability.

In the creative economy, the past is the currency. It pushes brands from production of new goods and services toward history, heritage and tradition. In story-mongering, a brand's old output is resurrected and the new output is enriched with motifs from the past in order to give them history. Today, for something to be modern, it needs to be archival.

Past also has a firm place in the creative economy. Unlike the previous economic models that depleted our physical world, the creative economy exploits time. Past is a reliable way of monetizing time (what worked once, is going to work again). "Anything that we are comes from our past," Miuccia Prada recently noted. "There is this discussion of nostalgia, but that's not at all the truth. We look at history to learn something. Taking a piece from the past is not conservative. It's liberating it from its cage."[10] Raf Simons adds, "You cannot talk about beauty without going to the past. You cannot erase the history of beauty, it is what defines our ideas of beauty today. We always go back."

It's lucrative to own time. As the ultimate currency, time increases price of something. Otherwise, we wouldn't have a saturated resale market. A reboot, a sequel, or a reissue also increases the value and the price of an original. Customers make a purchase with an eye on its future value in the resale markets. Dealers do the same. Thanks to their past, commodities turned investable assets with appreciating value.

In the economy that monetizes time, the ultimate goal is to achieve immortality. Kering, LVMH, or Prada bid to immortality through their foundations, which are part of the cultural economy as much as Louvre. Immortality is, however, best achieved when a brand monopolizes one's entire way of passing time. As Patrizio Bertelli formerly of Prada notes, "we want to it be a mindset, an experience centered around the Prada brand . . . Creating an identity that transcends what we sell."[11]

In this context, a narrative that surrounds products is often more valuable than the products themselves. Chanel Classic Double Flap bag has been a staple of every new and old money person who wants to signal their social and economic elevation. We want wearable "myth objects" to demonstrate our taste, insider status and cultural savvy. We don't want to be mere consumers. We want to be associated with game-changing moments, places and people. It gives us a new form of wealth, not by association, but of association. The more we get to associate ourselves with knowledge and creativity and cultural activity, the greater is our social distinction and higher our cultural status.

This duality – present and future value, social and economic one – turns an item with a narrative into an investment asset. Fashion pieces are being increasingly considered as assets and the rise of buy-to-flip customer persona keeps them liquid, and for a growing number of consumers, buying secondhand is the first choice. By 2025, global spend on secondhand clothing will reach $77bn, according to GlobalData, a research firm. Total spend on fast fashion is predicted at $40 billion, per the same source. Secondhand spending spread to antique shops, furniture, books and jewelry. The pre-owned luxury watch market is set to grow to $30 billion by 2025, per McKinsey. In May 2024, there were 182 million vintage hashtags on Instagram, compared to 38 million Gucci hashtags. Authentication is still the largest bottleneck in the luxury fashion marketplaces, but also the biggest opportunity for brands to build their own. Mulberry did exactly that, in the form of Mulberry Exchange, which finds new owners for their authenticated and restored classics. Cocoon, a luxury handbag rental site, mixes sales of pre-owned luxury bags with rentals.

In the past-driven economy, the wealth-mongers are archivists, curators, advisors, dealers and collectors who have the power to increase any past thing's value by linking it into a collection, curating it and remixing it with the current items and vibes.

This process is not limited to products. Buildings, neighborhoods, cities and regions all can be (and are) reinvented. A couple of years ago, a Chanel perfume advertisement leaned into an invented tradition of jasmine gardening in Grasse, where jasmine artisans passed their craft over generations. Lower East Side of Manhattan, High Line or Williamsburg have gone through numerous narrative filters. In the process, Grasse and Williamsburg acquired previously missing heritage and touristic magnetism.

Looking to the past is a lucrative shift. Economically, value is extracted over and over again without production costs. Culturally, value is created through democratization of collecting, curation and creativity, generating endless commercial opportunities. Socially, inequalities created by wealth and access are accompanied by the new ones (Who knows the story? Who doesn't?).

This is relevant. Creating new narratives around value that circulates in our economy transforms how this economy is organized and by whom. Social and cultural power is economic power – and the emerging social and cultural valuations override the value defined by editors, institutions and other gatekeepers.

Often forgotten, material history is the archaeology of trends. Knowing how to read it unpacks the dominant narratives of a time: Who got to participate in making of cultural products? Who was excluded? Which ideas and values were mainstream, and which ones were marginalized? Products are the excavation sites of culture, social mood, context and people who inspired them, created them, promoted them and made them possible.

This new knowledge of economic, cultural and social history impacts the cultural influence strategy. It transforms how we see and value things, and when we change how we buy things, we change what we buy. Archival reissues, vintage dealers and secondary marketplaces usher a new wave of talent into traditional fashion organizations: storytellers together with strategists, curators and merchandisers, archivists and stylists, collectors and designers, vintage dealers together with traditional sales channels. Here are five key considerations for brands on how to use the past right:

Invent a story. To exploit the past, a brand first needs to have it. If it doesn't, it needs to invent it. The purpose of inventing heritage and tradition, and their narrative enrichment and embellishment, is to create cultural currency. In the creative economy, cultural currency equals economic currency, and creativity is the mode of its production. Whoever has the best story, and the best way to tell it, wins. Best stories own time. They get to shape the narrative and define the history (see the movie *The New Look*).

A side note: DTC brands, from Away to Casper to Brooklinen, often fake their own origin story, turning a Harvard Business School homework assignment into a divine inspiration. Origin stories take time to reveal their own significance, and creating Muji suitcase knockoffs, super-charged by VC money and performance marketing, offers well-dressed commodities, but not brands.

The tendency of fashion brands to mine their own past for stories has been described by cultural publication *032c* as "the heritage problem." The term refers to newly appointed creative directors' habit to look into the archive and redo their brand's iconic heritage. The tendency may not be, by default, original, but it works. Tiffany & Co. recently launched a creative double-header, a campaign titled "With Love, Since 1837" and the Tiffany Wonder exhibition in Tokyo, both aimed at celebrating this brand's storied past. Kim Jones has been doing something similar since joining Fendi. Gucci, building upon its original Vault idea, launched the story of its loafer, made iconic not only because it is unchanged in time but because it has been a prototype for the Gucci brand.

Past-driven storytelling does not aim at originality (it takes time or something truly original to be created, and even more time for it to spread) and is less interested in ideas than in their biography. Biography of an idea, a person, or a brand gets dramatized and enriched, and we get Louis Vuitton transformed from a suitcase maker into an artist, Christian Dior into a hero in *The New Look*, and the Gucci family into a heightened drama in *House of Gucci*.

The key in inventing new stories based on the past is interpretative newness. The catch is that the new interpretations have to be trendy and constantly refreshed: the creative embellishment of history does not itself stand the test of time. This is why the members of the creative class who are at the helm of brands – like fashion designers, film directors, hoteliers, writers, luxury CEOs – are getting frequently replaced. To keep going, the story of the past needs to be constantly relevant in the present.

Interpretative newness makes storytelling circular. To get the always new angles, stories have to simultaneously traverse separate cultural areas and time through self-reference and copying. In the circular story-telling, reboots, sequels and reissues of an origination narrative are the main output. As the new Mad Max is ready to hit the movie theaters this summer, so are the late 1970s styles. In the age of reference, nostalgia is the mood.

Despite all of its reverence for the past, brand storytelling is ultimately disrespectful of it. The past that brands exploit had once been the future. Originality was such that it broke the confines of its present. Creatives whose biographies brands celebrate always looked forward, never backward. To make a story immortal, we need to give it a future by bestowing on it enough time to unfold in the present.

Capitalize on the past demand. Depletion of natural resources, supply chain challenges, and global competition forces brands to turn their profit-seeking to exploitation of things other than production and labor. A brand's past demand is a good predictor of its future demand. A few years back, Galliano's Dior saddle bags and logo monograms experienced an unexpected but quite powerful revival nearly 20 years after their original release. Wasting no time, Dior promptly revived both, to great success (and profit). Alternatively, secondary marketplaces provide an option to brands to buy and resell their own vintage items, powered by "product passports," and save on raw materials, labor and production costs. There's also a strong aspect of the original creativity behind the now-vintage items and how this creativity energized fans and culture alike that can be tapped into in the present moment.

Find your community. Reviving the past links a brand with its original fans and their stories. Little works better than nostalgia, across audience groups. In addition to its own archivist fans and collectors, there are archive, curatorial and vintage accounts on Instagram and TikTok for every era, style and subculture. Everyone seems to be a vintage dealer these days, and they are a great starting point for activating a brand's vintage collection. They are also a great source of inspiration, ideas, and preowned items. A$AP Rocky and Matthew Williams wear archive and vintage pieces that create a new subculture around them. Just like streetwear, vintage items have the power to create secret clubs of experts, obsessives and connoisseurs.

Remix. There are multiple scenarios in activating a brand's vintage collection. Isabel Marant Vintage is a separate destination from its main site. Madewell and Farfetch include resale link on their main sites. PRADA pre-owned items are sold on Vestiaire Collective, TheRealReal, Poshmark and their own site. But vintage collections work best when remixed and integrated with the current seasonal collections throughout sites and stores via merchandising, styling and visual merchandising. In this way, they drive cross-sell, expand audience base, give depth to products, inspire more creative styling, and link past to its present for stronger brand messaging. The fastest and easiest way to keep making money is through constantly creating new and different stuff by recombining the old.

Bide your time. There's such thing as a future vintage (Byronesque, a vintage reseller, is one example[12]). Creating future collectibles is for a brand a way to foresee (and strategize) its future relevance. What is present will soon be past, and there are next generation of curators, collectors, vintage dealers and archivists to feed.

Product icons

Nothing succeeds like success, the saying goes. The surest way to turn past successes into current success is by reissuing proven bestsellers and familiar designs. Burberry trench, Calvin Klein briefs, Stanley Cup and Gucci loafers are some of the examples of product icons that are able to sustain many iterations. Gucci loafer is so notorious, notoriously recognized, and rich in symbolism, that in 2023 Gucci rooted its entire collection in it (it was when Gucci was in-between designers, so the loafer was also a symbol of resilience and unity). Additional option is to create sequels of iconic products that build upon design of the original, giving both the sequel and the original a lift (like J. Crew's giant chinos, which are a sequel of J. Crew's signature chino).

Product icons are building blocks of the brand narrative. Through iconic products and their many interpretations and reboots, brands influence culture.

For Esprit's brand revival, we defined seven signature products, which were rooted in the brand's storied history as much as in the consumers' affinities in the present moment. These seven signature products – parka, chunky-knit, button-down, drawstring bag, soft suit, tracksuit, and soft skirt – were considered the purest distillation of the Esprit brand, and these were used to usher the brand into cultural relevance, many decades after Esprit's heyday. For the year after their introduction, these seven signature products were also the filter through which Esprit interpreted seasonal trends and made them its own.

For Banana Republic brand revival, I defined the "BR Look," a signature product vision, brand codes and aesthetics.[13] This product vision was accompanied with the new product design approach and process, which synchronized brand and product messaging on the annual basis, defined quarterly themes for both brand communication and product design, and executed the rollout in a manner that conveys these themes best. The "BR Look" has been codified in the form of a manifesto, as well as in the anchor products that were its backbone (a white oversized button-down, chinos, a leather jacket, a cashmere turtleneck, cargo pants).

Every brand, no matter the products it sells, should develop building blocks like these as it attempts to rebuild its brand. Even fast-food restaurants have signature products. McDonald's has the Big Mac, McNuggets, and Fries, but it struggled in the early 2010s because it attempted to expand its menu to appeal to a larger audience. In 2015, McDonald's cut its menu offering and focused on price and quality. This "less but better" decision helped lead McDonald's sales to exceed $25.49 billion in 2023 and its operating margin to increase to 52% that same year. Since its focus on core products, McDonald's market value has reached $197.37 billion.

Perhaps more important for brands than association with celebrity people is to create celebrity products. Louis Vuitton's Millionaire Speedy,[14] launched by Pharrell Williams, the brand's creative director, is meant to create halo around all (non-millionaire) LV's Speedys. Those who have a Millionaire Speedy know that everyone else knows how much they spent on it. The role of a brand's hero products is to be the purest distillation of the brand identity and values, a bridge between the brand heritage and its future, and the fodder for brand collaborations. Other celebrity products are Hermès Birkin, Chanel Double Flap, Gucci GG Marmont belt, Air Jordans, Mini Cooper, Volkswagen Beetle, iPhone, Big Mac, Lego building blocks, IKEA Billy Bookcase, Uniqlo Ultra Light Down, Rey-Ban Wayfarer, Calvin Klein briefs, Burberry trench, and so on.

Sometimes, products become iconic for a short period of time, turbocharged by social media and pop culture. Stanley is more than a hundred years old maker of hand tools, drink ware and other products, like camp cookware sets. In 2023, the Stanley Cup's popularity exploded thanks to a video that went viral on TikTok. The Stanley Cup has turned into an iconic product. Similarly, Miu Miu, a fashion brand, has been in recent years churning wearable memes, like micro-skirts, cropped sweaters and button-downs, and crystal embellished panties, which became much-imitated social media and real-world phenomena.

Product icons allow brands to capitalize on their own intellectual property. Pioneered by Disney and turbocharged in the recent years by Marvel and Mattel, the IP monetization model is spreading from entertainment to other categories, like retail. In retail, IP-driven growth strategy is to build, manage, amplify and monetize a brand's past and present intellectual property. Revenue comes from sales of iconic products but also through licensing fees, collaborations, product sequels and reboots, and partnerships.

Aesthetics

Shortly after his return to Apple in 1997, Steve Jobs called a meeting and lambasted his employees. "You know what's wrong with this company?" he asked. "The products suck. There's no sex in them anymore." This meeting is rumored to have inspired the invention of the iMac. In the first five months of iMac's existence, Apple sold 800,000 units, turning a profit of $309 million in 1998 and $601 million in 1999. The iMac marked Apple's return to profitability.

Throughout Gucci's 101-year history, this fashion brand's popularity has waxed and waned, and its business results have faltered and rebounded. What Alessandro Michele understood when he joined the brand in 2015 is the need for a strong and clear product aesthetic, along with a number of product icons, including Princeton Loafer Mule. This strategy worked until 2022, when, with changing geoeconomics and consumer tastes, Gucci entered a period of decline, culminating in the 18% sales drop in Q1 of 2024. Gucci still generates $10.8 billion USD in revenue as of 2023, and as of spring 2024, there is an intent to invest in Gucci's new creative director Sabato de Sarno's success. De Sarno puts forward the pared-down, more wearable, more nonchalant and effortless aesthetic, leading to increase of 144% of searches for Gucci. Fashion industry commentators foresee fast fashion brands like Zara copying a lot of de Sarno's aesthetic, propagating it to the mass market.

Apple and Gucci understood that a signature brand aesthetic is crucial to brand growth. The more defined the aesthetic, the more curatorial rigor it offers to design, merchandising, and styling, and the more it allows these functions to align in delivering a new, shared brand experience. A signature brand aesthetic translates into core products, which are the purest distillation of what a brand is. For Gucci, these products are GG Marmont and Soho bags, Princetown slippers and loafers, the GG belt, GG canvas print, and 1970s-inspired suits and dresses. For Apple, these building blocks are the Mac, iPad, iPhone, Apple Watch, and AirPods.

An entire aesthetic world is a lot harder to copy than visual handwriting or a tone of voice. It also takes longer to develop. Aesthetics is a value innovation form that stems from the brand POV. This aesthetic POV defines who the company is, what it stands for and also what kind of customers it wants to cultivate. It is a magnifying glass to view the world and as such, it can live in multiple expressions: as product design, store design, visual merchandising, sales staff, but also in the forms of content, curation and collaborations.

At Banana Republic, I defined "Imagined Worlds"[15] as the aesthetic territory[16] and "Expedition in Imagination"[17] as the brand promise. The entire brand creative output was guided by these two directions: brand campaigns, ecommerce photography, marketing campaigns, packaging, tissue paper, visual merchandising, styling, marketing collateral in stores, social media content and website design. Each season, a group of adventurers would go to an imagined world, on an expedition in imagination – and be dressed the part.

Signature aesthetics gives companies differentiation and durability. JW Anderson's pigeon and canary bags, art direction for its campaigns, and exaggerated concepts make it stand out in the saturated image economy.

Each season, Loewe's creative director, Jonathan Anderson, puts forward a collection with memorable aesthetic – be it a knitted full-length cardigan with no sleeves, ultra-high-waist pants, or shoes, socks and trousers fused together into a single item of clothing. Value innovation is not in having superior product properties or novel tech but in the emphasis on aesthetic experience (consider how GOOP-endorsed products have been accused of deceptive health claims yet continue to be popular). Successful brands ingrain themselves in the cultural context, not a market segment. Apple, Tesla, Aesop, Shinola and Hermès introduce new meaning in culture by linking aesthetics with their products. They create cult objects – Mac, iPhone, Tesla, Birkin – that serve as aesthetic totems. (Peloton advertising regularly depicts their bikes as cult objects in shrine-like settings.)

These days, aesthetics that emerges on Instagram and TikTok is emulated and appropriated by brands. The modern aesthetic influence goes in all directions. Mob wife, dark academia, coastal grandma, and eclectic grandpa have all sprang out of consumer groups and subcultures and have been turbocharged by algorithm. Brands' job is often to curate this aesthetic, incorporate it in their own designs and use it to dialogue with culture.

Aesthetic innovation infuses taste and meaning into the ordinary consumption. The most mundane products – like a lip gloss or a toothpaste – come with a considered color palette, details and logos. "Good business is good art," said Andy Warhol, and this may as well be the modern branding's mantra, fed by the massive offering of Instagram inspiration. Late Virgil Abloh transformed mundane objects (rugs, water bottles, T-shirts) into works of art through quotation marks. Before him, surrealists did the same. Today, shows like *Bridalplasty*, *Million Dollar Decorators* and *100% Hotter* tell consumers how to redesign their face, house and life. Aesthetic innovation gives competitive edge to consumers and brands alike: innovativeness is not in having superior products or new technology, but in a signature recognizable aesthetics. Successful modern brands create cult objects – GOOP's Jade Egg, Tesla Tequila, Nike Jordan 1, Bored Apes – that combine the aesthetic experience, identity building and social display.

Closely connected with a defined brand aesthetics is the brand look, executed through creative and art direction, talent selection and styling.

Styling

The most immediate expression of a brand aesthetic is the brand look. When Alessandro Michele took over as Gucci's creative director in 2015, he established the Gucci look: an androgynous, hippie, renaissance mix of florals and sequins, glamour and glitz, surprise and whimsy, subversion and creative expression, and accessories and prints that nod to equestrian motifs. While it has since fallen out of favor with consumers, this maximalist, neoromantic look is still instantly recognizable as quint-essentially Gucci on the street and on the runway. "I feel Gucci!" and "That's so Gucci!" are part of our cultural lexicon.

Establishing a recognizable brand look is the right thing to do: a signature aesthetic is crucial to brand recovery. When we were reviving Banana Republic, one of the first things I did was to define the signature Banana Republic look, with a clear styling codes, like double-and-triple belting, cinched waist, elevated materials, generous silhouettes, functional and dressy, and styled with and a lot of accessories. This styling has since been consistently implemented across Banana Republic's e-commerce photography, marketing and brand campaigns, and visual merchandising.

At the same time, brands are living and breathing things, in constant dialogue with culture. To keep exerting cultural influence, brands need to evolve with it. This means that a brand aesthetic needs to stay alert and sensitive to the shifting trends. The signature brand look is not set in stone: while it is necessary for it to always have a strong point of view and a defined DNA, it needs to be responsive to the cultural trends. One thing is to have a blueprint; another one is to have a dogma.

Michele's genius at Gucci was to capture cultural shifts before they were happening on the global scale – today, everyone from Timothée Chalamet in Haider Ackermann's red backless pantsuit to Brad Pitt in a skirt are sporting a version of the androgynous Gucci look pioneered by Michele and spread by Harry Styles and Jared Leto. But what made a brand exciting and successful in one cultural moment would not be as exciting (or successful) once it enters mainstream. A couple of years ago, we were one step away from the ruffled men shirts being sold in Zara.

A strong brand look gives a brand recognition, differentiation, consistency and loyalty. A strong brand look can also be antithetical to scale. The mode of balancing the two – a signature brand look with the brand growth – chart a company's business trajectory, particularly in mature markets, where brands cater to many different segments. A brand with a single-minded brand look cannot successfully capture all of them without losing some of that aesthetic conviction. In order to address different market segments and serve its market as a whole, a brand has to make its aesthetics clear but flexible.

There are multiple ways to do this:

Brand autocracies. Strong identities, especially when they are closely linked to the founder and the founder is still around, turn brands into autocracies. Ralph Lauren has kept his signature styling for many decades. It has been widely imitated, borrowed from, and culturally celebrated, but it doesn't move the stock price upward. Lacking the external financial pressure, Ralph Lauren doesn't need to move fast.

Lauren's brand look, although unchanged for decades, is still attractive to a specific taste community. This taste community keeps the brand afloat.

Diversification. Marc Jacobs created Heaven to play the 1990s role that Jacobs once had: to stay close to urban young generations and design for them. The main brand focuses on Marc Jacobs's creative vision when it comes to apparel and on archive revivals and core collection when it comes to handbags. Diversification is different from diffusion as the two brands have entirely different looks.

Talent turnover. Creative directors of luxury fashion brands change houses every few years. Michele left Gucci in 2022. By frequently changing their creative directors, luxury fashion brands keep reintroducing different creative interpretations of their core identities, keeping these identities fresh.

Diamond model of growth. Unlike the traditional luxury fashion pyramid model, in the diamond model, products and/or services at the bottom look differently but do not diminish in quality compared to those at the core. At the core, the diamond model features limited editions, special collections, small product series and/or limited distribution. The core has a more selective and/or controlled distribution than the entry level. The levels are all part of the same brand universe but adhere to the different audience segmentation criteria.

Brand codes

Brand codes refer to recognizable symbols that brands use on their products and in their communication. Brand codes can be a color, like Barbie pink or Tiffany blue. They can be design details, like the Chanel tweed or the Gucci double-G logo. They can be brand iconography taken from an area of a human endeavor, like tennis, horse riding or travel.

The role of brand codes is to provide narrative continuity for a brand and create familiarity with a brand in the culture. Brand codes create a rhythm in consumer expectations, and are constant over seasons and years.

At Banana Republic, I worked with Decade,[18] a branding agency, on the new brand system, including the logo, font (Banana Serif) and ownable color palette (Banana Yellow), with defined primary and secondary colors. Additionally, I was tasked with developing the print system for the brand, which has since been featured on the in-lines of coats, jackets and trenches, as well as pocket lining and dress prints. With Decade, we worked on developing the signature brand patterns to be featured on packaging and tissue paper and as brand accents on clothing (like stitched crests and detailing).

Brand codes are strong narrative devices. Today's consumers don't speak in genres, product categories, or gender. They speak in memes, references and remixes. This language of boundary-crossing and cross-pollination breaks down genres by default: it takes elements of different genres and turns them into a new cultural output. On the Internet, consumers are not buying something that belongs to a specific genre (e.g., tailoring); they are buying into a look of, for example, Timothée Chalamet, Pharrell or Tyler, the Creator. These looks themselves are memes that get to live on in the endless references they generate.

Through its brand codes, a brand participates in culture. Prada's famous triangle logo now lives in many iterations – as earrings, felt patches on the back of coats, or perfume bottles – and is inimitably Prada. Like secret society crests of old that people used to recognize each other as members of the same club, brand codes today function as "the mass produced secret," per New York Times critic Jon Pereles.

Without recognizable and defined codes, it is easy for a brand to get lost in culture. Having a system of brand codes ensures that a brand stands out in a fluid cultural landscape, where fashion genres – like music genres – were once upon a time a tool for companies to categorize, brand, market and promote themselves for decades. This tool is increasingly irrelevant to how consumers actually discover, buy, and wear fashion.

It is also increasingly irrelevant in how they express their status, identity and taste. Once, fashion genres like punk, preppy and minimalist used to mark a subculture and define one's identity, cultural affiliation, values, interests and social orientation. Now, the tables have turned, and a feeling of self defines genres. One-of-a-kind point of view gives one-of-a-kind personal genre. Breaking down fashion rules and recontextualizing fashion items has become a vehicle of signaling one's authenticity and difference. Before, we dressed to belong; now, we dress to stand out.

In this new fluid cultural world, where forms of creative expression – print, digital, textile and space – are merged, sneakers are the new loafers, comfort is king, and vintage plays are on the same pane as the latest season. What was once a niche (streetwear, vintage, gorpcore) is now mainstream. Old prep – and its exclusive and rarified nature – has nothing to do with the new prep: Rowing Blazers style their tailoring with hoodies, windbreakers, and body piercings. It is a far cry from Ralph Lauren's gilded American Dream, and that is precisely the draw. Aimé Leon Dore recently collaborated with Martin Greenfield, a Brooklyn-based bespoke tailor, on its formalwear. The result is a double-breasted tuxedo worn over sweatpants – equally suitable for a night out in a fancy restaurant as it is for a Saturday morning paper run.

Blame secondary fashion marketplaces like Depop where individual expression and experimentation made fashion genres obsolete by the very platform design. Popular looks are created by "regular" people doing creative things with their clothes, and this creativity is what we are buying: someone's look, not a particular genre within it. Everyone is a fashion curator, a creator and an influencer, and many fashion voices inevitably result in quicker trend cycles. People get bored and move onto the next look, making genres increasingly and irretrievably less relevant. Anything can be discovered, bought and sold everywhere, by anyone, and to anyone.

Self-expression as the ultimate fashion genre is intrinsically linked to our new social, psychological and cultural appreciation for personal identity, self-care and mental health. The feeling of self, and keeping one-self in regard, also merges fashion with other cultural forms, like music, film, art or food. Telfar expresses himself through his fashion shows that are theater, performance art, and a party.

Self-expression translates into products. Today's product icons – retro Jordans, 450s – are no longer reflections of social distance. They are cultural references with a promise of belonging, connoisseurship, and a shared identity. That and purpose are linked to our pandemic-induced questioning of priorities, values and our role in the world. Fashion today is less about established genres that brands represent and more about what brands stand for and are doing in the world.

On the other end of the purpose spectrum are style algorithms. Just as Spotify does in music, StitchFix and The Yes do in fashion: they learn our style and serve us personalized recommendations. But Instagram and TikTok go even further, though less overtly. Algorithmic person-alization of these platforms effectively obliterates fashion genres as it lets us enjoy highly appealing looks, regardless of who created them, where they came from, or how they were originally categorized. Looks are delivered based on algorithmically created style profiles rather than editorially.

Algorithms level fashion's playing field: we get to randomly discover niche categories of people, styles and behaviors. Trends that emerge in smaller communities get more easily and more quickly picked up by wider audiences; a niche lives (and dies) in the mainstream quicker.

The ability to bring things together from different contexts in unexpected ways has become the ultimate stylistic flex, no more reserved for celebrity stylists and artistic directors only but for everyone. What was once a conceptual exercise is now daywear.

Potentially the biggest feature of brand codes in the post-genre world is their stability amongst pop culture's openness to interpretation. If visual aesthetics is culture's grammar, then today's culture operates predominantly around words, a.k.a. brand codes. Like a DNA sequence or blockchain, the possibilities are endless. There are signifiers – physical and digital – that we recombine at our disposal without changing them. The blueprint is the person wearing clothes and the way they wear them. Just like an observer makes a great work of art, a wearer finishes the fashion narrative. Art is not in any of the objects; fashion isn't in any of the clothes. It's in one's own feeling of self and where they want to take it. Brand codes ensure that association is not lost.

Graphic design

Once upon a time, when an item sold too well or too quickly, a luxury brand would discontinue it. Hermès is still doing it, but examples are dwindling. In the modern visual culture, it doesn't even matter – photos of Birkins, Miu Miu crystal-embellished panties and rare Air Jordans are everywhere.

To participate in popular culture, a person doesn't even need to participate in any of its cultural markets: design, music, fashion, film, art. It is enough that they own, share and trade in cultural images. As the scenarios outlined here show, culture is migrating toward ever more imaginary – literally and figuratively – from bizarrely imaginative fashion designs that are bound to do well on TikTok to images that are consumed as the real thing. This migration doesn't come as a surprise: memes, references, recontextualization and cultural symbols are the Internet's language that got to dominate culture as well. These new formats gave rise to even newer formats – performances, resales, shared closets and sartorial weirdness – that turn luxury into commerce via culture.

Jean Baudrillard, a French philosopher, would be thrilled. Forty years ago, he suggested we have "replaced all reality and meaning with symbols and signs, and that our experience is a simulation of reality.

The distinction between reality and representation vanishes. There is only the simulation, and originality becomes a totally meaningless concept."[19]

One can argue that reality, symbols and society now have an inverse relationship. In the fall of 2021, at the height of cryptocurrency and blockchain craze, Balenciaga launched its Afterworld collection in *Fortnite*. Since then, Balenciaga's print ads featuring Justin Bieber look like they came straight from *Fortnite*. (Baudrillard would have called this "the third order of simulacra," where the representation precedes and determines the real.)

Culture has always been in the business of simulation: of making its stories believable by the massive numbers of people. Through this simulation, Coco Chanel has been turned into an artist and Louis Vuitton into a craftsman, Ralph Lauren is about American aristocracy, and Möet Hennessy has been made according to a secret recipe transmitted over generations. People believe a brand is valuable because others believe it is valuable; the more we believe something's valuable, the more valuable it becomes.

Graphic design is the ultimate expression of signs and images that a brand wants to project. It is a blueprint for a brand world and all the brand's modes of communication, from products to retail spaces to websites and social media to events and experiences.

Graphic design has a great aspirational power, which fuels the modern economy, where the growth motor doesn't come from physical products but from the story-rich, visually powerful intangibles like a print, a pattern or a pixelated cartoon character.

Graphic design powers the business and brand growth in the following ways:

Monetizing IP. Turning graphic design into a new revenue stream is directly monetizing a brand's intellectual property. Archival prints, patterns, font and other graphic design elements can all be reissued, and used as a fodder for collaborations, partnerships and merch.

Fighting off commodification. Having a solid graphic design system allows a brand to cultivate "elitism to all": it can sell a lot of items to a lot of people without diluting a brand's symbolic value. This symbolic value makes a commodity incomparable and gives brands a temporary monopoly by rendering their competition irrelevant.

Collaborations. Brands use graphic design to give themselves cultural meaning and relevance. Endowed with recognizable graphic design elements, products stop being commodities and become works of art, by sheer association with the story and heritage of the graphic design that has been deployed.

Co-creation. Graphic design is a strong co-creation platform. Peter Saville, a graphic designer, co-created Lacoste's iconic crocodile logo with the brand team to celebrate this brand's 90th anniversary. The results are a collectible and offer a brand multiple cultural hooks.

Identity. In mature markets, graphic design is one the brand's key product differentiators. A brand makes products stand for something more than their function and separates them from commodities. A strong graphic design system enforces brand identity, ensures its continuity and connects products, packaging, tissue paper, retail experiences and a brand's digital properties into one narrative.

Membership. Graphic design turns consumers into brand members: those who want to be seen wearing a Burberry check or Chanel tweed or Air Jordan original color combinations.

Taste communities. Graphic-design-obsessed communities often follow a brand thanks to its brand system. A recognizable graphic design is a strong motivator for brand purchases, loyalty and affinity. There are curators and collectors in this group, as well as those who associate with the brand purely on the visual plane, without buying a brand products, but responding to its aesthetic.

Marking an occasion. Brands spend inordinate amounts of money and time to mark holidays, centenaries or other notable events, when a limited-edition, scarce graphic designs to do the trick. The easiest way to commemorate an anniversary or a special occasion is to invite a collaborator or a creator to play with a brand's famed graphic design elements, like Lacoste did.

Physical retail. Graphic design extends its life through digital and physical wall treatments, galleries and physical renditions in the form of packaging, card, marketing collateral or tissue paper.

Retail experiences

Opening of a new store leads to an average 37% increase in overall web traffic for brands, according to International Council of Shopping Centers.[20] Biased or not, the study confirms what marketers know: the halo effect is real, and investing in physical retail is today cheaper than any of the performance media buys.[21] According to the research from the Business of Fashion Insights, a think tank, 31% of luxury shoppers visit stores on a monthly basis, with 68% preferring in-person customer service that physical stores provide.[22]

First to discover this were online-first brands of the past decade, furiously opening new stores (see the stretch of Spring Street in NYC between Lafayette and Broadway). From now-troubled Glossier to Allbirds, this block is a testament that nothing is still more cost-effective in customer acquisition and long-term loyalty than physical retail. The catch is to never again think of your physical store as a sales and distribution channel.

In traditional retail, a core user activity is a product purchase. This activity maps closely to how the retail business is monetized: to increase product purchases, retailers expand their footprint by opening more stores and featuring more products.

Today, a product purchase is not a core user activity. Instead, what's core to users may be participating in a community, having access to high-quality lifestyle content, benefiting from personalization, attending events, identifying with an aesthetic POV or a social message, enjoying VIP membership perks, or experiencing a superior delivery service or a celebrity connection. Most successful retailers today monetize their businesses around these activities. Their business models do not revolve around their products, and their physical stores reflect this shift.

An example is Dior's newly renovated store on 30 Avenue Montaigne, which represents this brand's entire universe: a permanent museum, a restaurant, three gardens and an apartment where guests can spend a night. Another example is Pharrell Williams transporting his Pont Neuf set from his first runway show as the creative director for Louis Vuitton menswear into three stores, in New York, Los Angeles and Hong Kong. Each of the stores features part of Pont Neuf, adorned in gold and mirrored checkerboard. A bookcase opens a secret accessories room.

The most successful brands design their stores around consumers' pattern of engagement with a company. Here are some of the more popular ways retailers create, deliver and capture user value with physical stores:

A lifestyle center. For a lot of consumers, shopping is losing its clout. In its place are exercise, travel, home decor, nutrition and identification with a social cause. This is the new ammunition for personal currency. Stores like Goop or the newly opened outpost Dover Street Market in Paris trade in this new currency by displaying a full-blown lifestyle, as well as the values, beliefs and motivations that underpin it. Together, they are tangible and shoppable demonstrations of a specific social point of view.

Consumer intelligence hub. By understanding how consumers move in-store and interact with merchandise, a company can optimize its physical space – including the way it designs and displays its products and the level of service it provides – and interpret consumer behavior on a more personal level. This understanding translates to a better customer experience. Thanks to data obtained in its pop-up in NYC's Brookfield Place shopping center, Warby Parker discovered that customers deem trying on prescription glasses in public too intimate but that they had no problem testing sunglasses.

Social clubs. For a long time, retail brands were built by editors, spokespersons and brand managers. Today, they are built by fans. Modern brands simultaneously build upon what's already out there in their fan networks, and they use these networks – be it Instagram, WhatsApp, WeChat or a local coffeeshop – to test and spread their ideas. Rapha, a cycling brand, and Tracksmith, a running brand, have clubhouses, for example, which are inspiring meeting places for cycling fans. They serve as stores, cafés and hubs for races, rides and events.

Visual retail. Along with turning their stores into immersive and interactive theme park-like journeys, retailers like Winky Lux and Glossier invest in creating viral experiences with a high novelty factor. The central idea is not that visitors will go to the store to buy something; the idea is that they'll heavily Instagram it so their friends will want to visit and buy something. By emphasizing the overall social experience of discovering, buying and using the product, Glossier bakes referrals and sharing into all of its physical properties.

Retail everywhere. This strategy expands retail from stores into hotels, Airbnb apartments, co-working spaces and standalone accommodations. A Ma Maniére is an Atlanta-based men's streetwear retailer that, in addition to its three-floor store, offers a "living concept" next door. Customers can rent an apartment fully equipped with A Ma Maniére products, including clothes, furniture, kitchen appliances, decorative objects and tech.

In addition to the fully fledged, long-term physical retail locations, brands across categories are opening temporary retail experiences/event spaces.

Ever since a disgraced but still not unpopular Ye launched his first New York pop-up in Soho back in 2013, the neighborhood has been a holy grail for temporary retail formats. It's combination of attractive permanent retailers and year-round high foot traffic make it perfect to reintroduce the brand into a market, showcase a collaboration or convey a brand point of view (and more). The key to a pop-up's success is to consider it strategically, through combination of real estate and retail data, and as a way to connect their audience development, marketing, data and merchandising, and sales.

Pop-ups make a lot of sense at the time when retailers are restructuring their fleets: they are a relatively cost-efficient way to test a new market before opening a permanent physical store. Having a physical presence benefits online businesses, and contrary to the long-held belief, it doesn't cannibalize online sales. It allows consumers to discover and try products before they buy them. Pop-ups are a cheaper way to acquire customers than Google and Meta ads.

As the pop-up landscape matures, consumer fatigue and market saturation with "immersive," Instagrammable destinations force retailers to explore how having a pop-up store ladders up to their brand and business. Successful pop-ups today are not a sole PR play and/or a sales and distribution channel. They succeed because their role is defined in relation to the overall brand and business strategy and in terms of "jobs to be done" for a retailer's audience.

In retrospect, they adopt one or more of these approaches:

When introducing a New Product. Back in 2011, in the pre-pop-ups era, Andrew Kessler, co-founder of creative agency Article Group and author of "Martian Summer," opened a book store. Called "Ed's Martian Books," the book store featured only one book – his own – and drew wide attention of media and passersby. Today, this approach has been adopted by Dirty Lemon in their Tribeca Drug Store or Heatonist in Williamsburg. Louis Vuitton Virgil Abloh menswear pop-up this summer similarly celebrated Abloh's Fall 2019 collection for the brand, and featured limited-edition range of day-glow accessories designed exclusively for Chicago. To announce launch of its new scent, Byredo opened a camping pop-up that brought the scents of countryside to the center of Paris. This single focus strategy can successfully be applied when an established and/or multi-category brand ventures into a new product line or category.

When entering a new market. This strategy has been adopted by the Copenhagen-based brand GANNI, which has been present in the US market mostly through online and offline wholesalers. They have recently opened a pop-up modeled after Danish Kiosk stores, featuring a selection of limited-edition GANNI ready-to-wear and accessories, mixed in with locally sourced products and snacks, all curated by GANNI's creative director Ditte Reffstrup. Far from being just a cute way to bring Copenhagen vibe to New York, GANNI store is a low-risk path to its potential permanent retail presence in the New York market. Pioneered by Bonobos some years ago, the approach links online audience demand and sales data with merchandizing and tests demand in the limited-time, cost-effective way. Recently, this strategy has been adopted by Lord & Taylor to re-enter New York City, opening a limited-time pop-up in Soho a year after closing its Fifth Avenue flagship.

When showcasing a collaboration. Currently one of the most common pop-up formats, it's perfectly captured by Supreme and Louis Vuitton celebrated their "ultimate fashion partnership" with a series of eight pop-ups across New York, London, LA, Miami, Paris, Seoul, Beijing, Sydney and Tokyo. Hodinkee similarly partnered with Omega to launch a ten-day pop-up store in Soho, featuring Omega's Speedmaster and Seamaster collections, all available for in-store purchase. Venture a bit further, and there is a number of food/fashion pop-ups, like Heineken's collaboration with A Bathing Ape that included T-shirts, outwear and matching beer carriers, all sold at Japanese restaurant Izakaya in East

Village. Uniqlo collaborated with eight Japanese ramen shops, including Ippudo, for a T-shirt line.

When demonstrating a company's values. In 2019, Patagonia opened its Worn Wear pop-up store in Boulder, featuring "gently worn" apparel and a new upcycled product line. Worn Wear initiative is a tangible expression of company's values of sustainability and its dedication to preserving the environment, as well as a perfect way to cater to hardcore outdoor enthusiasts who take pride in wearing vintage Patagonia pieces. In New York, bedding brand Parachute and apparel brand Cuyana teamed up for a pop-up based on mutual admiration and shared values of quality and customer-centrism.

When offering a service. Rent the Runway partnered with W Hotels, offering guests the option to rent pieces of clothing when they book their rooms, waiting for them when they arrive. Beyond this latest iteration, hotel pop-ups have also long been staples of DTC and established retailers alike, looking to expand their audiences beyond the current customer base.

Entertainment

Joerg Koch, founder of *032c*, a cultural publication, noted that fashion "has become an operating system across all modern business . . . you need fashion to communicate cars, real estate, and experience, among other things."[23] He concluded, "fashion has a become a force for entertainment."

Independent production and distribution studio A24 would agree. Since its inception more a decade ago, it has been known as "the internet's greatest merch store."

Just as Marvel has its cinematic universe, A24, *032c* and a growing slew of fashion brands are building their own creative universes. A creative universe is a tangible expression of a brand's vision and promise: it connects a brand's core business with the hype-making activities, like merch, collaborations, memes, content and creator partnerships. A24 gives its collaborators a platform for the creative conversation long after the movie is complete (like makeup palettes inspired by the beauty looks of characters in A24 productions); Miuccia Prada does something similar with *Women's Tales*, an anthology of short films by female filmmakers. Jonathan Anderson, creative director of Loewe and JW Anderson, both styled Luca Guadagnino's movie *Challengers* and produced a short with this director for Loewe.

The purpose of creative universes is to – through its narrative, characters, aesthetics and products – intertwine themselves with culture and its conversations. In the mega-universe of culture, there are a lot of galaxies that intersect. Nothing works better than a product that is also a wearable meme, a shareable image, and a piece of merch, all in one life-span. (Think Victoria Beckham "My Dad Had a Rolls-Royce T-shirt" or JW Anderson's pigeon bag).

Critical for building a creative universe is to connect up all areas of cultural production into one galaxy: film and gaming, fashion, art and design, tourism and branding, architecture and content creation, style and social media, storytelling, performance and music, advertising and publishing are all part of a single brand's galaxy.

Creative universes are expansion of brands' aesthetic vocabulary and are increasingly synonymous with the culture itself. Patrizio Bertelli, the former CEO of Prada, notes that he sees value in "creating an identity that transcends what we sell. We want it to be a mindset, an experience centered around the Prada brand . . . After all, the definition of luxury nowadays is quality of life in every aspect, including what we eat, how we travel, the art and culture we have access to, and what we wear."[24] Prada successfully combines art, design, food and fashion in the recognizable Prada creative universe.

In spring 2024, Gucci released its "Gucci is a feeling" campaign to capture the brands movement toward our becoming used to describe our emotions, moods and ways of spending time.

For Gen Z, shopping is the top among their entertainment activities (above playing video games), per Business of Fashion's annual State of Fashion report. Indeed, these days, majority of the cultural output seems to be a performance and a stunt. MSCHF's 99 fake Andy Warhols or their Wavy Baby shoes. Balenciaga fashion show, set in a snowy, windy tundra. Twenty-four-hour live Telfar TV. Corteiz Bolo street performance art dubbing also as its community's exchange of luxury brand jackets for their own worn puffers. The early precursor of fashion-as-performance is Vetements, with its pop-up show in Hong Kong and subversion of everyday brands into luxury items. The peak of consumerism as performance is Ye x Julia Fox's "Date Night," leading into Yeezy Gap Engineered by Balenciaga collab. Life mixes with culture mixes with art mixes with commerce.

Increasing number of culture-savvy brands is crossing into entertainment. LVMH, a luxury conglomerate, recently launched its entertainment venture 22 Montagne, aimed at producing movie and television content linked to its brands and partnering with Hollywood talent to tell its brands stories. Nike's Waffle Iron Entertainment has already been in the content production business for some time, and Kering, a luxury conglomerate, has bought a stake at CAA, a global talent agency.

In the context of entertainment, marketing becomes creative production. The majority of contemporary creative production does not aim at originality. It takes time or something truly original to be created, and even more time for it to spread, and is less interested in ideas than in their biography.

Biography of an idea, a person, or a brand gets dramatized and enriched, and we get Louis Vuitton transformed from a suitcase maker into an artist, Christian Dior into a hero in *The New Look*, and the Gucci family into a heightened drama in the *House of Gucci*. The catch is that the creative embellishment of biographies does not itself stand the test of time. By design, these interpretations are meant to be trendy and constantly replaced by new interpretations of the same heritage and tradition. This is why creatives who are at the helm of brands – like fashion designers, film directors, hoteliers, writers, luxury CEOs – are getting frequently replaced. To keep going, the creative economy needs interpretative newness.

Interpretative newness makes creative production circular. To get the always new angles, creative production simultaneously traverses separate cultural areas and time through self-reference and copying. In the circular creative production, reboots, sequels and reissues of an origination narrative are the main output. Get ready for Dior Part VII.

In addition to the ever-closer ties between different areas of culture and entertainment, entertainment as an approach changes the way brands market themselves and their products. Quirky and fun snippets of always-on content now complement seasonal campaigns and big PR pushes, merch and product are mixed with brand communication and messaging, and creative collaborations ensure novelty.

Seasonal product releases and campaigns around them are now also amplified through a considered rollout schedule, which mimics a movie release more than a traditional fashion collection calendar. Hype-building starts with teasers, trailers, opening nights, VIP events and launch. Product releases are teased through content and merch prior its launch to drive interest.

The more a brand invests in content, experiences and entertainment, the more differentiated (and valuable) its products and services are in the mind of consumers and the easier it is for a brand to sway their preferences. To turn their brands into entertainment, CEOs need to invest in creating and capitalizing on their brands' intellectual property.

By default, all brands are intellectual property. At the time of their founding, brands were an idea, an inspiration and a (real or imagined) need they addressed. Yet they are still managed as retail, not as entertainment.

The original intention behind Apple was to change the way people viewed computers, making them small enough for everyone to have them in their home, thus spurring human creativity. Phil Knight's original idea for a running shoe company was to tap into the cheaper – but still high-quality – Japanese shoes, which he imported and sold out of his car. Dick and Mac McDonald failed in the movie business and focused on drive-in restaurants, selling 15-cent hamburgers.

Everything that brands do can be monetized as intellectual property, from their origin story, to signature products (e.g., Nike's waffle trainer), to their logo, color palette, prints and patterns (e.g., Chanel tweed), tone of voice, slogans and jingles, advertisements, founders, fan fiction, myths and sagas.

The *Michelin Guide* started in Clermont-Ferrand in 1889 as a way for the Michelin tire company to encourage more tourists to take car trips (and wear their tires off), at the time when there were less than 3,000 cars in France. The guide originally included information like maps, tire-changing and fuel-filling manuals, and rest stops, but over time it started including lists of hotels and restaurants. The Michelin categorization of restaurants became exceedingly popular, and the company hired mystery diners (food critics) to anonymously dine in and review restaurants, assigning them stars.

Brands are entertainment with products and services attached. In addition to creating content of the value for consumers outside of a company's core offering, like Michelin does, further strategic approaches are as follows:

Support an area of culture. This spring, Loewe announced the winner of its sixth annual craft prize. This Spanish brand is known for its leather craftsmanship, and with its prize, it expands its positioning into culture, supporting emerging craftsmen. Loewe gives modern craftsmen a global platform and recognition, through showcasing the shortlisted projects during NYC x Design, at the Noguchi Museum in Queens.

Partner with established entertainers. These days, McDonald's is not anymore in the hamburger business.[25] Instead, it is in the show business. This new positioning is enforced by the company partnering with Travis Scott, across food, fashion and community efforts. McDonald's recently launched Scott's signature order, the Travis Scott Meal, on McDonald's menus. The collaboration further includes custom apparel (hoodies sell for up to $500) and a charitable component. Beyond fast food, luxury fashion brands already tapped into providing branded weddings for celebrities like Sofia Richie (Chanel) or Kourney Kardashian (D&G).

Broaden your brand purpose. IKEA stopped defining itself as a furniture company and identifies now as a source of "affordable, well designed everything." Broadening a brand's purpose allows it to expand its core business into new categories (in case of IKEA, these are sustainable energy, scent, merch, apparel, gaming). Pictured: IKEA x Byredo scents launch, titled "What does a home smell like?" Restoration Hardware expanded its empire to private jets, yachts, restaurants and hotels, in addition to their core furniture offering.

Brand everything. From products to experiences, everything can be branded. Tiffany & Co., thanks to its history, legendary cultural status and recognizable blue color, can collaborate with anyone. The result is constant novelty and instantly recognizable output, from Rimowa x Tiffany to Daniel Arsham to Nike and Supreme. Additional examples are the Karl Lagerfeld hotel in Macau, Fendi Private Suites, and Brunello Cucinelli's branding of Solomeo and its famous pasta meals.

In a brand's creative universe, the entire brand toolkit comes together: merch, collaborations, archive reissues, product icons, aesthetics, styling, brand codes, graphic design, retail experiences and entertainment. Each of these creative executions amplifies and augments one another, and synchronized, they together create a brand's recognizable cultural frequency.

Notes

1 https://www.trillmag.com/life/food-drink/balenciaga-releases-1750-chip-bags/

2 https://key4all.com/

3 https://ultimateparticipationtrophy.com/

4 Eden, C. (2024, July 10). Retrieved August 2024, from https://fashion culturesparsons.wordpress.com/author/huanc673/

5 Pearson, A. (2024, January). Retrieved August 2024, from https://www.linkedin.com/posts/andyisacopywriter_the-future-unboxed-dielines-2024-trend-activity-7135762691515674624-OFbI/?trk=public_profile_like_view

6 Andjelic, A. (2020, August) Retrieved August 2024, from https://andjelicaaa.substack.com/p/dj-model-of-ikea

7 Thompson, D. (2017, February). Retrieved August 2024, from https://www.theatlantic.com/magazine/archive/2017/01/what-makes-thingscool/508772/

8 https://www.gq.com/story/banana-republic-vintage

9 https://www.stoneisland.com/en-si/archive-prototype-research-series.html

10 Chitrakorn, K. (2024, February). Retrieved August 2024, from https://www.ft.com/content/a651379c-e2d6-4614-b084-2129cef16aa0

11 Sciorilli Borrelli, S. (2024, March). Retrieved August 2024, from https://www.ft.com/content/ccb5a32d-be04-45f3-92f5-2b8ffaa0a45b

12 https://byronesque.com/

13 https://andjelicaaa.substack.com/p/the-new-american-look

14 *Hypebeast.* (2023, December). Retrieved August 2024, from https://hypebeast.com/2023/12/pharrell-louis-vuitton-millionaire-speedy-bag-what-makes-worth-million-dollars-analysis

15 https://www.andjelicaaa.com/imagined-worlds

16 https://www.andjelicaaa.com/the-new-br-look

17 https://www.andjelicaaa.com/2021-holiday-campaign

18 https://decadenewyork.com/

19 Baudriallard, Jean, Simulacra & Simulation, The University of Michigan Press, 1984

20 https://www.icsc.com/news-and-views/icsc-exchange/icsc-halo-effect-study-finds-physical-stores-drive-increase-in-online-traff#:~:text=NEW%20YORK%2C%20October%2015%2C%202018,to%20a%2037%20percent%20average

21 https://www.snowflake.com/resource/retail-and-consumer-goods-data-ai-predictions-2024/?utm_source=google&utm_medium=paidsearch&utm_campaign=na-us-en-nb-retl-phrase&utm_content=go-rsa-evg-eb-retail-and-consumer-goods-data-ai-predictions-2024&utm_term=c-g-retail%20media-p-692431458157&gad_source=1&gclid=Cj0KCQjwmt24BhDPARIsAJFYKk3S2ffKt_jmnK7TqF6g2_j9gnVHiDxSaceziZ9zwkpZRkOBep1goDQaAgEKEALw_wcB

22 https://www.helpscout.com/75-customer-service-facts-quotes-statistics/

23 Koch, Jeorg, 032C Issue #44 – Winter 2023/2024: "EDGLRD", 2024

24 Sciorilli Borrelli, S. (2024, March). Retrieved August 2024, from https://www.ft.com/content/ccb5a32d-be04-45f3-92f5-2b8ffaa0a45b

25 https://www.economist.com/business/2020/11/12/takeaways-from-mcdonalds-remarkable-comeback

Media amplification

3

Media amplification maximizes influence of a brand's cultural products, synchronizes the impact of these products into a narrative and creates a cultural frequency for a brand.

Brands used to influence the mainstream culture through their advertising on mass media, like TV, print, billboards and public relations. Today, they influence culture through the cultural products they create: content, merchandising, collaborations, events, aesthetics, experiences, archives, history, entertainment, fandom. Rather than on the mass audience, media plans are directed at subcultures, taste communities and consumer niches. Through media planning, brands tell their story.

Media amplification inserts a brand's cultural products in variety of cultural contexts. In some of these contexts, a brand's cultural products will flourish; in others, they won't get noticed. Cultural products and media amplification always go together. Without media amplification,

DOI: 10.4324/9781003534907-4

cultural products will stay niche; without cultural products, media is blindly increasing click-through rates without augmenting the brand's cultural influence. Through cultural influence, companies build their brands and grow their business.

These are the core tenets of media amplification:

Short-term and long-term. Media amplification delivers both short-term and long-term results. For some cultural products (like collaborations or content), the results can be delayed; for others, like experiences or events, they can be more immediate. Media amplification works on different timelines with different cultural products – some are easier to amplify than others – and with different cultural audiences. Calvin Klein's Jeremy Allen White Instagram campaign[1] was a cultural product that had impeccable cultural timing – a few days before the Golden Globes, where White received his reward, and going into the compressed awards season. Media amplification went from an Instagram video to a full-blown campaign. In contrast, the campaign of Desigual, an apparel brand, with Hari Nef[2] has remained in the Instagram videos-seeding stage and hasn't been since amplified. Calvin Klein's cultural influence was immediate, with 40 million views on Calvin Klein's Instagram account and 86% of YoY brand engagement increase. Sales influence is longer-term. During the period where Calvin Klein exerted the high immediate cultural influence, its stock fell 20% and sales in North America dropped 8% YoY.

For the sales to catch up, Calvin Klein has to keep the cultural influence going (and not wait until the next awards season).

Story. For a media amplification to work, brands first need to have a coherent and resonant story. "You can have the best technology, you can have the best business model, but if the storytelling isn't amazing, it won't matter. Nobody will watch it,"[3] noted Jeff Bezos. A clear brand story internally unifies the organization and streamlines the decision-making. It unifies product and brand messaging. It directs merchandising and retail experience. Most critically, a good brand story guides which creative products are developed and outlines their rollout and their media amplification strategy.

Customer segmentation. Media amplification assesses customer segments based on their potential to grow a brand's cultural influence in a way that generates the greatest financial returns. Not all audience segments will have the potential to generate cultural influence, and brands need to prioritize cultural products for those who do. To select key audience segments, companies first need to operationalize their brand goals: Do they want their cultural influence to drive awareness? Increase differentiation? Achieve brand relevancy? Or drive brand desirability? Cultural influence strategy – the way a brand story is told through cultural products and amplified through media – will hit different segments differently, depending on a company's business goals.

Framed as amplification of cultural influence, media buying and planning become a creative exercise. This creative exercise revolves around identifying all the different cultural contexts for a brand to participate in. When a brand is present across different cultural contexts, it can be nimble and reactive to unexpected cultural shifts, like the sudden wild popularity of Stanley Cup of the emergence of various TikTok aesthetics, like dark academia, tomato girl, or mob wife.

Structuring media planning as a portfolio prevents customer deadlock, where a brand repeatedly targets the same customer. Media plan's job is to recognize cultural conversations, trends and emerging aesthetics and use them to amplify a brand's own cultural products. A recent example is how Away, a luggage retailer, spoofed Calvin Klein's Jeremy Allen White's ad by dressing their own luggage in Calvin Klein briefs and photographing it on rooftops, with a witty social media copy.

In contemporary culture, there isn't one big cultural moment. There are a lot of cultural moments. The success of a media plan depends on how many of these cultural moments a brand can capitalize on, amplify or create. IKEA, a furniture company, frequently spoofs Balenciaga in a perfectly timed manner. Their recent social content around towel-skirt featured Balenciaga version of the skirt together with an IKEA towel. Immediately following Met Gala, IKEA did a similar cultural commentary by featuring a model resembling Doja Cat, a singer, wrapped in a white towel, on an IKEA parking lot (Doja Cat was widely featured wearing only a towel prior to Met Gala).

Media amplification connects a cultural product like an Instagram video with another cultural product, like merch, with the third one, like a retail experience or an event. In this way, media amplification creates a self-driving loop of cultural influence. Telfar, a fashion brand, turns its fashion shows into performances, collaborates with established brands, features its community on its Instagram feed and has a regular entertainment programming in the form of Telfar TV. All these examples show how well Telfar knows its audience and the cultural contexts for the brand. More importantly, Telfar focuses its media on amplifying its own content.

Media amplification addresses culturally multi-contextual nature of the cultural influence strategy, and allocates investments that go from mass to niche to content product to instant conversation.

The three tiers of media amplification are:

Top tier

What: Seasonal mass media brand campaigns (print, OOH, non-linear TV buys, influencers and events, sponsorships). Merch and hero products are also in this tier.

When: 4×/year

Why: Brand awareness, interest and consideration

Middle tier

What: Digital brand and marketing campaigns, brand content (editorial, marketing and product), brand channels (top- and mid-funnel), including affiliate marketing, website, email, social media, digital video, high-impact digital units, sponsored content, product placement and all other digital media buys. Email and CRM programs.

When: Ongoing

Why: Brand awareness, interest and consideration, loyalty

Bottom tier

What: Social content and social commerce, including live-streaming, shopping videos and reels, and Instagram and TikTok commerce; bottom-funnel media buys (programmatic, SEO and SEM, product-driven paid social, membership and invite-only events, loyalty programs).

When: Ongoing

Why: Conversion

All tiers of the pyramid work in sync, building a brand's continuous presence in culture and providing a portfolio approach that ranges from mass to targeted media tactics. Always-on entertainment content is mixed with seasonal campaigns and media pushes. Awareness and consideration are a backdrop for more targeted marketing actions, like conversion, retention, advocacy and loyalty: they provide a constant stream of new customers. Through portfolio approach, a brand renews its customer base, without falling into the customer fatigue trap.

The idea behind the new media plan is to create and maintain the narrative universe for the brand. Media are non-linear and focused on building a narrative world, through a continuous streams of media activity (rather than seasonal bursts and bottom-funnel media tactics). Additionally, the new media plan approaches a brand as a revenue driver (vs. a cost center) and buys media in the way that capitalizes on a brand's own IP (content, products, retail experiences, events, merch, archive reissues, collaborations).

This new media planning approach is easier to understand if framed as the media amplification of cultural influence. Even the big buys on the top of the pyramid are teased out thought paid teasers and trailers, announced through merch and selected hero products and finally released together with in-store experiences and events, like movies. The rest of the pyramid is nurturing fandoms, celebrates brand products, provides always-on entertainment and maintains a brand's cultural awareness and emotional resonance.

When selecting their strategy of media amplification, brands should first define their short- and long-term goals, their investment in achieving these goals, and their expected return on this investment. Then they should select the strategy of cultural influence that is best going to deliver their expected ROI.

A big part of the process of selecting the strategy of cultural influence is to assign KPIs to its three components: (a) story, (b) cultural products and (c) media amplification. The role of these KPIs is to:

- Define impact that the selected strategy of media amplification has on revenue.
- Define financial contributions from each of the cultural products and media amplification tactics.
- Justify a given investment, in particular cultural products and their media amplification.
- Work toward predictive and/or retrospective scenarios that link brand actions with financial performance.
- Manage creativity for profit and growth.

Connecting cultural products with media amplification tactics and audiences, accompanied with the goals and KPIs, allows a brand to link its cultural influence strategy with the financial results and is an improvement versus the traditional brand marketing approach and metrics. In the media amplification approach, each cultural product is augmented with a specific audience, through specific media tactics.

Each has financial metrics, as well as the contribution to the overall brand story.

Interstitial storytelling

Brand stories are today best told through interstitial storytelling, which refers to a series of narrative bursts that are connected into the web of a wider story. A story is told in series, with each piece of content containing germs of the next story and ending with a cliffhanger.

For brands, this means marketing their products like movies, starting with teaser trailers, then trailers, then marketing activations, with the role of building anticipation for a collection release, rather than marketing a collection once it is available.

Anticipation

Powered by interstitial storytelling, anticipation is based on narrative discovery. A teaser and a trailer drive narrative discovery of the movie they promote. Video game levels and challenges drive narrative discovery of a game world. In retail, anticipation is the result of the narrative discovery of a collection, a brand vision, or a collaboration or partnership. But more than an actual collection, of interest is the anticipation itself, powered by sneak peeks, previews, leaks, teasers and trailers in place of campaign videos. The wait is the game; a collection is less important than the content announcing it.

Fragmentation of taste

Mass brands face a challenge of not only putting forward an irrelevant style or the obsolete set of values. Their challenge is that there is no longer one predominant set of values or style. Consumer tastes are ever more niche. Consumers gravitate toward communities and brands – or both – that cater to their niche tastes. Telfar, Aimé Leon Dore, Tracksmith, the Frankie Shop and Alo Yoga are some of the examples.

In the micro-taste communities landscape, mass brands come across as too generic and superficial. The winning growth strategy is to go deep and narrow and to achieve scale and wide reach by aggregating niches.

A media portfolio caters to niches is built around (a) hobbies, lifestyles and interests, (b) price, (c) channels, (d) perceived benefits (status and prestige, health and wellness, affordability) or (e) values.

Each product and messaging mix in the media portfolio focuses on a specific type of customer and gives them the superior selection of choices within that vertical.

In the media and entertainment sector, this growth strategy allowed Netflix to create a global market made out of niche taste communities. Thanks to personalization, Netflix is able to reach the mass audience while keeping product differentiation in its entertainment portfolio. Just as my Netflix is not the same as yours, a single mass fashion brand cannot meet diverse market demand unless it's operated as a portfolio.

Post-icon age

The 1980s had Benetton and *A Nightmare on Elm Street*. The 1990s had grunge and *Pretty Woman* and Britney Spears. We now have Y2K, "re-editions," "inspired by," "brought back" and "in collaboration with." We also have anti-icons, like Ye or Musk or Adam Neumann, who are as known for their antisocial antics as for their creativity.

The problem is not the crisis of originality. Iconic products or ideas or personalities are always outcomes of their context. The mood has to be right for everyone to like chunky sneakers or shoulder pads. When the media, culture or retail were mass, so were the social symbols. These days, we'd be pressed hard to find symbols that mean the same thing to everybody. The geography of influence, taste and communities shifted to micro. The big, sweeping planes of culture that asked for big, sweeping products and personalities are replaced with many micro cultures, each with their own niche products and personalities. Our concepts of "cool" and "iconic" are forged in the intimacy of our own taste communities.

At the same time, the taste space has never been flatter. Burning Man outfits, family pajama sets, Halloween costumes, weddings, craft breweries and coffee shops all appeal to our tendency to revert to the recognizable and the familiar. Just like crickets or lightbulbs, only amplified with Instagram likes, Twitter hashtags and other performance metrics, our taste signals are harmonized, so all of us end up looking the same, dressing the same, liking the same things, and visiting the same places that also start to look alike.

Here are the five forces that ushered us into the post-iconic future:

Newness

Icons take time to build a myth around themselves, and our culture operates under compressed trend cycles. When the pace for coming up with the "next thing" quickens, the best bet in creating something iconic is to riff off on something that's already iconic (cue tireless Air Jordan reboots). The irony here is that, under pressure for newness, brands don't really create anything new. Similarly, driven by desire for newness, consumers never really get anything new.

Popularity

Cult movies were often commercial disasters. They became iconic despite or, more likely, due to their lack of commercial success. Not anymore: commercial success dictates what's created, so we get endless repetition of popular things. Everything, from movies to sneakers, is a sequel.

Memeification

Everything's a meme, a commentary on the already familiar, popular and recognizable things, which are changed just enough (3%) to be taken out of their original context and turned into a joke or an ironic read.

Strategies of enrichment through invented heritage and ratification also belong here.

Productivity

Most productive designers are proclaimed iconic: Coco Chanel and then Karl Lagerfeld, Maria Grazia Chiuri, Demna Gvasalia, and until he opted out, Pierpaolo Piccioli. In their hands, an original idea oversaturates culture. It can be argued that Elsa Schiaparelli's and Rei Kawakubo's contributions were greater, but less culturally insistent and pervasive, and less mainstream.

Death of a critic

Critics of lore used to be commercially impartial commentators dedicated to the artistic "truth." Today, a critic is part of the culture-media-commerce machinery that feeds itself. A person can change something "just 3%" and count to be overhyped by mainstream media and celebrities. In return, they are happy to become readily available content creators. Faced with this culture-media-commerce hype cycle, consumers get bored quickly and move onto the next thing. See the section discussing newness.

Portfolio-building

When going to market with their products and services, brands often tend to go all-in on one creative direction. While understandable, this strategy increases a risk for a brand when entering a new, untested, market and appealing to the new, unknown audience.

Rather than having one big bet with a cultural influence push – from sports to furniture to evening wear or beauty – it's better to have a lot of smaller ones.

Take sport for example: if a brand wants to enter this market, ideally it would create many doors in; serve diverse audience; and cover the entire fashion sports market rather than just one aesthetic (e.g., horse riding or tennis).

A more successful approach is to take design codes from a number of sports disciplines – racing, skating, dance, boxing, soccer, tennis – and filter these codes through the signature brand aesthetics (its look) in the context of sports.

In addition to preventing one sport to overwhelm the brand aesthetics (as is the case with Tory Sport), the mix of design cues from multiple sports opens the door for original remixes, collaborations, partnerships and content. Why focus only on influencers and creators in one sport, when you can work with many?

To avoid the brand schizophrenia, it is critical here to obsessively apply the aesthetic filter of a brand. Chanel Sports – regardless of which one it is – needs to have recognizable Chanel design codes. It is the same for, e.g., Hermès Sport or Aimé Leon Dore Sport. The outcome is a collection that is both versatile and consistent; it is in service of a brand look, versus the brand look shifting with a sport.

Different sports lend inspiration, creative expression, and unique heritage and history (e.g., a history of female soccer is different – and no less rich – than that of motorcycle racing). The appeal of this richness and diversity hits a broad audience (there is something for everyone), while serving the core purpose of a sports collection: to be worn when exercising, lounging or as leisurewear.

Sports today, regardless of a brand, hit the continuum between amateurs and professionals and appeal to sports fans everywhere. A brand endorses a number of sports disciplines, together with their communities, narratives and aesthetics. It's the shortest path to market domination, and the best strategy for mature markets.

Mature markets have many different segments, which a single brand cannot successfully capture without losing its identity. In order to address different market segments and serve the market as a whole, a creative portfolio builds multiple presence and differentiates a brand offering.

These differentiated offerings meet market demand in a more personalized way than a single mass brand can. Through a portfolio approach, a brand increases its hold on the market and fends off new market entrants by putting forward a full range of offerings (tennis, soccer, racing, dance, athletics).

A brand portfolio is a platform for a potential roster of new and emerging designers, brand collaborators, and creators, each bringing forth their aesthetic and design sensibilities. A brand portfolio approach encourages intrapreneurship, where teams are freer to innovate, test against consumer preferences and renew a brand's relevance and differentiation.

A brand portfolio is held together through curation. Curation is applied at the level of online and offline stores, in marketing messaging, but also throughout the entire value chain, in the selection of suppliers, producers, designers, collaborators, content creators, influencers and brand partners.

A clear in-store narrative and the thematic, frequently changing offerings aim to create harmony across the entire portfolio and make it feel like a coherent whole. As Rei Kawakubo told Dezeen in 2018: "I want to create a kind of market where various creators from various fields gather together and encounter each other in an ongoing atmosphere of beautiful chaos."[4]

This is a good model, and it does not limit a brand's portfolio just to new categories. It presents a brand – and any new category it chooses to invest in – as a tastemaker and a cultural voice. It allows brands in its portfolio to move faster, transmit future trends and taste, and not be followers of existing tastes and trends.

A brand portfolio is also hard to imitate because they now belong to a curated aesthetic world and have a strong cultural association. Curation protects the entire portfolio's pricing power and profit. Curation becomes the core product that a house of brands is selling.

Benefit of a portfolio is that it categorizes a brand offering. A portfolio both gathers the choices and reduces the number of options that the consumer faces, preventing the negative effects of the choice overload. It also organizes options in a nimble and responsive manner. If some parts of the portfolio are underperforming, they can be fixed or liquidated faster, without jeopardizing the house and the rest of its portfolio.

Activating fandom

A brand portfolio is matched with the media portfolio. For contemporary brands, it is not enough to have customers. In order for them to grow and stay relevant, they need fans.

Fans are going to watch every teaser and trailer and go to Reddit to decode signs and chat about a brand with others. Fans are a brand's biggest driver, as they create the right mood for the new ideas, products and looks to spread. SSENSE, a retail website, is made for fashion fans – connoisseurs, hardcore followers, in-the-know shoppers – who are going to get every reference and recognize every obscure image. The fastest way to attract new brand fans is to activate its already existing fans, and let them do the word-of-mouth work.

Fans can turn anyone into an icon. TikTok is a place where consumers spend majority of their time thanks to highly appealing content, regardless of who created it. There's no need to follow anyone or browse or search: content is delivered based on an algorithmically created taste profiles, where any of us can be potentially propelled to momentary iconic status, thanks to the fans' collective taste powered by a personalization algorithm. With TikTok as a blueprint for the modern culture, icons today are only personifications of a trend, not its creators. The mood has to be right for everyone to like full lips or a lot of Botox or Onitsuka Tiger Mexico, and "iconic" personalities, products or ideas are always outcomes of their context. A few years back, the most liked photo on Instagram was a picture of an egg named Eugene. If the mood is right, anyone can become an "icon of X," and if it isn't, no one can.

Audience strategy

When thinking about who they want to reach and speak to, brands often think of their audience in terms of their current and prospective customers: people who are either buying a brand's products or using its services or will so in the future.

But at any given time, a brand has a much wider and more complex audience of cultural observers, fans, customers, commentators and collaborators. It needs to build a relationship with all of them:

Observers. A brand reaches observers when it does something that the wider culture pays attention to. Observers are usually reached when a mass brand does a collaboration (e.g., Dunkin x everyone, McDonald's x Travis Scott, Ikea x Byredo, and countless other collabs). In addition to collaborations, observers are also reached through working with celebrities, cultural micro-actions, like a revival of a brand's archives, a brand refresh (e.g., Brooks Brothers) or an anniversary event (e.g., Ralph Lauren's 50th and Michael Kors 40th anniversary). If a brand manages to tap into observers' specific cultural obsession (vintage, affinity toward celebrities), they may become fans and customers. To keep them interested, however, a brand needs to keep constantly feeding the observer's cultural interest. This is an unlikely scenario. Still, the main benefit of observers is to widely spread the word about the brand.

Fans. Fans connect with a brand on a social level. They identify with a brand's values, appreciate its aesthetics, enjoy its tone of voice and/or seek to be part of its community. Fans may strive to, or occasionally, buy a brand's products, but the products aren't the basis of the connection. Examples are Gucci and Balenciaga.

Customers. Customers are interested in a brand's products and purchase them either for commercial reasons (price) or stylistic reasons (design, fit) or to fulfill a particular need (performance, occasion). Brands of course have customers that purchase it for the social status, and those customers are also dubbed as fans and observers.

Commentators. Commentators have the most impartial relationship to a brand and are most likely interested in it if a brand does something interesting per cultural observers and collaborators. Commentators also take interest in the brand if it pushes the boundaries of its category, market or the business model.

Collaborators. Collaborators join forces with a brand often due to it being a creative challenge, an inspiration, artistic exercise or a renewal of relationship with culture or to expand their audience and grow their business. At all times, a brand should keep the audience of potential collaborators in mind as collaborators are the way of attracting all other audience groups, outlined earlier.

A brand that regularly converses with observes, fans, customers, commentators and collaborators – its entire audience portfolio – has relevancy and staying power; a brand that speaks only to its customers does not.

In addition to the audience strategy that takes into account the entire continuum of those who influence culture, there is a more specific subset of audience segments defined through their consumption behaviors. There are at least four audience types that a brand speaks to at any given time.

These types are connoisseurs, superfans, selective buyers and skimmers. Each of these audiences is relevant for a brand, but they have different motivations, levels of knowledge, tastes, and reasons for interacting with it.

These four audience types are distributed on the scale–influence continuum, with connoisseurs being the smallest but the most influential group, and skimmers being the biggest group but with the least influence. Best brands address all four of these audience groups; successful brands talk to at least two.

Traditionally, brands focused mostly on selective buyers, who gravitate toward the trendiest, most popular, latest and greatest items. The new brand strategy focuses on all four groups, where each is ranked on its importance for a brand and the value it brings to both the bottom line and a brand's popularity.

How many of these audiences, and which ones, a brand addresses, defines its growth model, product and brand strategy, and its marketing activities.

The four consumption behavior categories are as follows:

Connoisseurs. Connoisseurs love the unique. NFTs, sneakers, jewelry, Japanese denim, places to go out and new music to discover are the lens through which they see the world and themselves. Consumption is a matter of their identity. Their preferred cultural domain – fashion or art or design or literature – is their mode of expression. They are informed, knowledgeable and opinionated and actively seek out new designers/writers/artists in order to be able to influence their social graph. From brands they expect the latest and the greatest information, discovery, uniqueness and differentiation. They mix their shopping with content from critics, curators and creators, who help them evolve their taste and provide a continuous stream of inspiration and new discoveries.

This consumer group can make creators, curators and brands big, thanks to their social influence, taste and following. They do not invent new trends, but amplify the ones that are bubbling up through writing, commenting, remixing, posting and wearing them, thus lending the emerging trends wider attention and legitimacy. Connoisseurs are critical for brands as they are their canary in their coal mine: they show brands where the culture is going and allow them to tap into trends before they become big. In return, connoisseurs get access, status, bragging rights and ammunition for their personal brand.

Connoisseurs' behaviors revolve around carefully curated Instagram posts and reels, TikTok commentary, a newsletter, a podcast and having an agent, and they know about new MSCHF drops before anyone else.

Connoisseurs are influenced by social media direct messages, a curated Instagram following, exclusive text groups, obscure magazines, deep-cut Tumblrs (!), boutiques, happenings and friends across the globe.

Superfans buy anything from a brand they are obsessed with. Sports fans and dedicated followers of brands like The Row or designer Phoebe Philo are in this category. A lot of brands, like Porsche or Rolex, brand everything from residential buildings to the Oscars green room to appeal to (or create) superfans. Brand extensions usually serve this purpose, when a brand builds a universe that spans many categories and experiences, like Ralph Lauren does.

Superfans are a valuable source of income for a brand, as they spend more, and more frequently than other customers. They are behind brands' VIP programs, exclusive events and invite-only clubs.

Outside of a brand, superfans do not have the scale and scope of cultural knowledge and are sensitive only to trends adjacent to the brand(s) they love (quiet luxury in case of the Row and Philo and less quiet luxury in case of Porsche). Superfans' focus is narrow and deep, and their knowledge often encyclopedic when it comes to seasons, products, materials, or looks. From their brands, they expect a close, exclusive and personal relationship: a brand is likened to an extended family, a hobby.

Superfans love head-to-toe looks and home designs that reflect their favorite brand, personal relationships that go beyond transactions, being the first to know about new releases, and preferential treatment.

Superfans are influenced by VIP service associates, boutiques and private message groups, brand ambassadors and brand events.

Selective buyers have time, attention and money only for the best of everything. Vintage lovers and hypebeasts are in this category, and they use their social graphs, content, places and events to lead them to the latest and the greatest. They love an area of culture, like sport or vintage fashion or sneakers, but – unlike connoisseurs – have a life to live. Their purchases are less a reflection of their identity than a flex and status signaling. Selective buyers rely a lot on connoisseurs to filter things out for them and present them with great things. Still, selective buyers are important in the brand ecosystem as they are ready and willing to spend money.

They appreciate brand events (if they have time to attend), casually consume brand content (if it is popular) and remix different parts of culture. This last feature makes them valuable, as they are the ones who solidify multiple trends and ensure they become mainstream. Thanks to selective buyers' consumption, brands benefit from the halo of their popular product/campaign/look/celebrity. Selective buyers are also primary consumers of brand merch.

Selective buyers are one step ahead of the mainstream, the latest drops and special editions, merch, things that reflect cultural moment, and being at the right place and the right moment.

Selective buyers are influenced by TikTok creators and Instagram influencers, a mix of specialized but high-quality newsletters, and the best of TV and movies.

Scrollers are everyday buyers with everyday taste. To them, commerce is entertainment and downtime, like video games, movies, and YouTube and TikTok videos. They don't think about their purchases; they just enjoy them. Simplicity, ease, novelty and entertainment are keywords. They are not brand-loyal, they gravitate toward the most popular, trendy and entertaining content, and they do not use their consumption to express their identity, status, or anything else. They simply want to have fun.

Shopping, brands, products and content are a reassuring backdrop to their lives and how they feel connected with the world. Scrollers are "tourists" in late Virgil Abloh's language, and do not get brand references and insider jokes and information (nor they aspire to). They scroll while doing other things (riding in an Uber, watching TV, being bored at work).

For brands, Scrollers are relevant as they make their brand mass and have potential to migrate into one of the first categories presented earlier. Unless they convert, however, they are low value, performance media-acquired customers, and a "general audience" for the brand.

To reach them, brand needs to make part of their cultural output simple, easy to understand, entertaining and trendy (but not too edgy). Like fast food, content needs to taste good, even if it doesn't have any nutritional value.

Scrollers gravitate toward anything mainstream, popular, trendy, seasonal and copy-paste. They are influenced by anything that's trending.

All of these audience types – connoisseurs, superfans, selective buyers and skimmers – expect entertainment from their brands. This trend toward entertainment is pushing brand executives to dust off their content studios, acquire movie-making chops, maniacally collaborate and start putting showbiz talent teams together.

But the exact entertainment strategies are still work in progress.

Entertainment means not only traditional long-form TV and movie content and amusement parks but also short-form social content, snippets of dance routines and cultural commentary, paparazzi shots, events, capsule launches, and merch and retail experiences. Pharrell understands this entertainment portfolio well. At LV, there's always something happening in between runway shows – which themselves are spectacles – either a new store opening (the LA one gathered an impressive crowd of celebrity guests) or a capsule, like the recently released one with Tyler, the Creator, or a celebration event for a capsule. The outcome is a lot of cultural interest, owned and shared content, and the global attention management that no other brand can emulate.

Entertainment is, in this moment, an approach and an attitude, rather than a specific set of tactics. It focuses not just on the big event/launch/release/show itself, but on the time in-between. In fashion, it is still relatively rare to have always-on media outside of the seasonal fashion calendar, and media plans revolve around big buys mixed with performance marketing.

The strategic shift is a matter of survival. Media is going through the great repricing, where market corrects the costs of traditional advertising, like print and TV, as well as of paid digital media. From consumers' point of view, media is valuable if and when they respond to their social needs, identity markers like status signaling and belonging, motivations, tastes and interests. But since there are 912 million ad-blocking users worldwide in Q2 2023, advertising's current role in consumers' lives (other than annoyance) are minimal.

The task here is strategic, not tactical. The starting point is specific customer profiles, their entertainment and information needs, influences, current barriers to purchase, and motivations. From this starting point, media planning teams have to focus on the key touchpoints in their customers' journey and shape their strategy around both unmet needs and unrecognized barriers to purchase.

In the entertainment-driven brand world, media focus is on the entire customer experience that a brand delivers rather than a media channel mix. Media plan is then driven by the architecture of the customer journey through the brand experience (online and offline, functional and social). This architecture connects individual interactions in a way that creates value (information, entertainment, socializing, etc.) to the end customer. The way individual interactions are connected becomes a brand relationship – the way a brand is experienced for a specific consumer group and thus key for brand's performance and growth.

Brand desirability varies among different customer groups (e.g., the same brand has a different temperature for commentators than for fans). Consequently, different stages of the customer journey have different relevance for a brand relationship with this customer group.

Imagine three customer personas: one younger and more trend-driven and price-sensitive, another functionality- and comfort-driven and less price-sensitive, and yet another status-signaling-driven, not price-sensitive at all, interested in quality and superior fit. In addition to influencing the product pyramid and brand actions, these three customer groups influence media planning as well. Persona-driven media planning prevents customer deadlock and moves budgets from retargeting and promotions toward strategic brand communication.

In the first scenario, this media plan targets customers that are most likely to belong to the first persona described: someone who is not brand-loyal, who is looking for seasonal items and who is gravitating toward the lowest price. These customers are least valuable for the brand as they usually do not convert into repeat customers.

Media amplification is tasked with driving brand consideration and evaluation in this customer group, through hooks that balance product information and brand creative. Commercially, focus is on product features to quickly drive sales. Media engagement revolves around actions aimed at increasing brand visibility and product relevancy for a wide group of trend-and-deal-seeking customers. The key engagement action is to get on their radar and to quickly drive traffic to commercial destinations, through purchase triggers.

In the second scenario, media plan targets customers that are most likely to belong to the second persona described: someone who is looking for functionality and comfort, less price-sensitive and more brand-loyal, and the most likely of the three to make repeat purchases. These customers are the most valuable to the brand and the source of its continued income.

Media amplification is tasked with driving brand evaluation (and re-evaluation) and with creating triggers for product and brand engagement and consideration. Commercially, focus is on communicating both brand and product value through owned content, brand experience online and offline, and customer service. Media engagement revolves around aspirational tone of voice, photography and aesthetics, and visual handwriting. With this target, the key brand behavior is the opposite of "take money and run" (that is more suitable for the first target). Service, personalization and value-adds through content and functionality invite repeated visits, loyalty and community.

For the more affluent, less price-sensitive, and more status-seeking consumers, there is a third scenario that revolves around brand evaluation and product purchase. In the brand evaluation stage, it is critical for a brand to convey what it stands for: its promise and values and aesthetic world.

Media amplification is tasked with conveying brand differentiation in terms of product and positioning. Commercially, focus is on product quality, fit and design. Media engagement revolves around actions aimed at creating and retaining this customer segment's interest through entertainment, content, social currency (influencers and creators) and styling (looks). To achieve this, a brand needs always-on, continuous presence across all customer touchpoints (social media, email, website, stores, paid media).

Notes

1   https://www.instagram.com/calvinklein/p/C1rjOR4uGg2/?hl=en& img_index=1

2   https://www.instagram.com/desigual/p/C4WKw7NtlbQ/?img_index=1

3   D'Onfro, J. (2015, July). Retrieved August 2024, from https://www. opensourceceo.com/p/jeff-bezos-deep-dive

4   https://somethingcurated.com/2016/03/22/new-address-same-name-inside-the-new-dover-street-market/

The creative class 4

Strategy of cultural influence assesses customer segments based on their relationship to popular culture, and their potential to grow a brand's cultural influence in the way that generates the greatest financial returns. It then creates cultural products and media amplification plans to realize this return.[1,2]

Cultural products are carefully rolled out in sync with selected creators, commentators and curators in order to better manage both brand and creator's fandoms and amplify the cultural influence. Cultural products are selected based on their audience. Cultural context needs to be right for the commutative advantage to take hold and for the cultural influence to become financially lucrative for a brand. Not all audience segments will have the potential to generate cultural influence, and brands needs to prioritize cultural products for those who do.

DOI: 10.4324/9781003534907-5

To select key audience segments, companies need to first operationalize their brand goals: Do they want their cultural influence to drive
awareness? Increase differentiation? Achieve brand relevancy? Or drive
brand desirability? Cultural influence strategy – the way a brand story
is told through cultural products and amplified through media – will
hit different segments differently, depending on the company's business
goals.

A March 2024 McKinsey & Co., a consultancy, study of aspirational
luxury consumers concluded[3] that there isn't a one-size-fits-all strategy
for this consumer group. Aspirational luxury consumers are defined
as "cluster of spenders who both helped fuel the luxury boom post-
pandemic but then contributed to its stall as they cut back spending,
resulting in lower sales growth for major brands, the aspirational luxury
consumer is many different people."

Due to their trend-driven spending, aspirational luxury consumers are
important in a brand's cultural influence strategy. A large part of this
group is sensitive to cultural moments, conversations on social media,
and actions of celebrities, creators and influencers.

Even more important than aspirational luxury consumers are members
of the creative class. Members of the creative class are cultural creators,
curators, critics, imitators, dealers and hangers-on. Examples of the creative class are photographers, fashion designers, stylists, hair and makeup

artists, influencers, writers, chefs, interior decorators, jewelers, furniture designers, florists, filmmakers, publishers, journalists and artisans. They play an important role in the modern aspirational economy, as they move ideas around, propagate narratives, make connections, assign value to things and direct wider consumers' attention, time and money toward aspirational things, places and ideas.

No consumer decision is made in isolation from its context, and members of the creative class influence this content through their own cultural output and its management and consumption.

For the creative class, there is no distinction between work and non-work, and its members spend innumerable hours creating economic value through their cultural output. This is their bargain: in exchange for being able to shape their job descriptions, flexible working hours and who they work with, creators have to constantly produce fresh cultural products.

For all the freshness of their cultural output, creators don't make much new. Their actual output is interpretation and recombination. They accumulate cultural capital through commenting, repurposing, reinterpreting, reviving and/or criticizing the past and current culture. In this pursuit, they often venture out of their territory and look for inspiration in the tradition of other disciplines. Kim Jones' FW 23/24 has been inspired by TS Eliot's poem "The Waste Land." Grace Wales

Bonner found inspiration in James Baldwin's work. Being a Renaissance woman or man these days is a matter of necessity: to stay relevant, creators need to keep riffing.

The creative class sifts through and reactivates the past with the purpose of creating something modern and new but powered by nostalgia and heritage. The idea here is twofold: familiarity, repetition, and recognizability are mixed with newness provided by the modern context. The original (past) intention is given enough of a difference to be considered fresh. The goal is to simultaneously deliver familiarity and surprise.

Cultural revivals and reinterpretations are often trendy; if JW Anderson creates a wearable pun, so will Louis Vuitton, Gucci and others. If the 1990s are trending, everyone will remake and reissue their classics (e.g., the Stam bag at Marc Jacobs). If surrealism is working for Daniel Roseberry and Maison Schiaparelli, other brands will give it a nod or a few. The newness and difference last only for a second until others catch on, forcing the originator of the difference to move on and come up with something new.

The creative class secures both continuity and newness of culture and plays a critical role in the modern economy as it directs consumers' time, attention and money toward aspirational things, places and ideas.

Belonging in the creative class is aspirational in itself; in the social and professional hierarchy, members of the creative class occupy a privileged position that does not adhere to social and corporate structures and behaviors. They are free to shape their job descriptions, teams, working hours and attire according to the parameters of their self-expression rather than any external rules and expectations. The freedom notwithstanding, being part of a creative class is a full-time job. In addition to having to perform in their respective creative fields (design, fashion, criticism, curation, writing, etc.), they also need to stay atop new trends and happenings, see and be seen, negotiate their fees, review contracts and self-promote.

The creative class achieves their coveted position of freedom and influence through either their talent, wealth, education or social pedigree (or a combination of the four). Regardless of the source of the creative class's prestige, keeping it is precarious. Directing people's attention, time, and money is enabled by creators themselves being brands. A member of the creative class is at the same time a merchant and a merchandise: they are packaging, selling and promoting themselves.

This self-referential dynamic applies to even the most prominent members of the creative class. Just as they need to constantly reinterpret and reinvent the past and present it as something new, they also need to constantly reinterpret and reinvent themselves. This is why members of the creative class are always on the lookout for a new creative territory to venture into and to use to differentiate themselves. Being a Renaissance woman or man these days is a matter of necessity: to stay relevant, creators need to keep moving.

Members of the creative class gravitate toward a cluster of creative expressions, ideas, experiences, places and things that both unite them and differentiate them from each other and everyone else. The politics of the creative class aesthetics is that never stand out in an obvious way but to be immediately noticed and envied. It has to be aspirational: others need to wonder where a member of creative class acquired this particular piece of clothing (Osaka? Shoreditch? Milan?) or heard about a particular book or a movie. Differentiation is in the details visible to the insiders, never in-your-face.

The reign of the great amateur

Members of the creative class range from professionals to amateurs. The latter do not identify with the anachronistic meaning of the word. Amateurs are not dilettantes or laypersons. They are not aspiring professionals either.

Amateurs are taste machines

Transport this taste-making sentiment to streetwear, watches, luxury fashion or any form of collaboration between them, and one would be hard-pressed to miss an amateur changing the rules of the game. Teddy

Santis, Dapper Dan, Kanye West, Virgil Abloh, Raf Simons or Hedi Slimane are all fashion amateurs. Simons studied furniture and industrial design. Lotta Volkova, largely credited for Vetements' and Balenciaga's look, is a fashion stylist. West's background is in music. Self-taught artist Helen Downie, a.k.a. the Unskilled Worker, is synonymous with a good part of Gucci's aesthetic. Downie, as her Instagram moniker suggests, is an amateur.

Thanks to their passion bordering on nerdiness, they keep brands alive and move the culture forward. The proto-amateur Jean-Michel Basquiat began as a street artist. Andy Warhol trained as a commercial illustrator, but this didn't stop him from working in sculpture, films, silk screenings and paintings that are today one of the most coveted and expensive works of art.

Japanese otakus, once referring to hardcore anime fans, frequently featured in William Gibson novels as trendsetting cultural obsessives, and with a good reason: Tokyo emerged as a global cultural lab during the economic boom of the Japanese late '80s bubble economy. Famously, stores of Bape, Undercover and Pinkhouse were dubbed as gathering spots for street artists, DJs, city pop clubbers, skaters and zine makers. The brands themselves were the forerunners of future trends thanks to their mix of global influences through their niche perspective.

Rewind a decade back, and New York City's it girls of the 1970s, like Anya Phillips, were amateurs of that era: they were stylists, photographers, muses and avant-garde movie actors, all at once. Phillips didn't have the patience for academic education at Parsons, where she was admitted. She honed her skill among trendsetters and artists of the downtown scene.

The flex of interpretation

Amateurs play a central role in the modern creative economy. They generate brand value through the process of interpretation. Amateurs' goal is not to create anything new, but to interpret existing ideas, trends, styles and looks by making them slightly different from before. Amateurs put things out in the world to be questioned, commented on and criticized: their MO is to experiment by collective trial.

Through their interpretation, amateurs save brands like Gucci, Louis Vuitton or Air Jordans from being outdated. Gucci Ghost's tagging gave Gucci a fresh economic context and enhanced its value. It's also regarded as something less calculating and utilitarian, and more sincere and countercultural, than if it came from a fashion professional.

Interpretation is a powerful cultural engine. Amateurs' genius is to reactivate the past in a way that is simultaneously surprising and familiar: Gucci bags live in many interpretations, depending who the collaborator is. Chrome Hearts, Off-White™, Heron Preston, Suicoke, or A-Cold-Wall* all make their mark by combining the recognizable and the slightly different. Like jazz or streetwear, it's a repetition in many forms.

Fandom meets creativity

Amateurs are free to endlessly interpret culture, heritage and brands because they're not bound by tradition, education, training or an established way of doing things. They comfortably reside in the domain of their own geekiness and play with things for fun and their own pleasure and status in their community. Theirs is the liminal territory between the "real jobs" and a hobby. Fashion stylists, who are today one of the biggest Hollywood power players, weren't considered as practicing an actual job until the 1990s.

Japanese denim otakus know more about denim stitching, washes, cuts and materials than most fashion editors or even denim-making brands. A denim amateur is the real expert in their encyclopedic know-how of trends and styles because they simultaneously appreciate denim and consume it. Like hypebeasts and sneakerheads, they're the prime example of knowledge in practice. They create, apply and influence cultural taste because they invest their time into finding the inspiration, often in their own social network.

This combination of knowledge and community places amateurs at the intersection of the fan and the creator. As fans, amateurs follow. White Claw fans bond over Etsy cowboy hats and ugly holiday sweaters, continuing the tradition of fan fiction and fan art. Media scholar Henry Jenkins wrote in *Textual Poachers*,[4] his ethnographic account on fandom, that amateurs' output "is a source of creativity and expression for those who would otherwise be excluded from the commercial sector."

To make sure that they fully participate in the commercial sector, amateurs cultivate a following. Self-promotion that often goes with the creator economy is a necessary narrative vehicle that either celebrates an amateur's style or their own personal story (Kanye is an example of both). The narrative guarantees continuity of the output, but it's also a savvy business move. It ensures that the work keeps coming in and that price premium is attached to it. Unskilled Worker made a name for herself that today comes with a considerable monetary value.

That's the genius of an amateur: they play in the loosely integrated cultural space outside the mainstream, all the while enjoying its full market benefits. Anti-professionalism doesn't equate anti-capitalism. They are beyond a simple economic dichotomy of romantic bohemians versus utilitarian professionals. They are better described as fans and creators.

This fan, or creator, cycle is endless. Amateurs are fans of trends, brands and styles and also part of the scene they influence and draw inspiration from. Fashion stylists, which didn't exist 25 years ago, are the creative directors of today. Instagram influencers are taking their place and becoming stylists, and (nearly) anyone can become an Instagram influencer. They all trade in the currency of taste.

The amateur economy

In the modern economy, stuff is cheap. Status comes from interpretation of culture and the resulting social capital. The entire streetwear and beauty industries rest on the shoulders of amateurs, who first went to Supreme, Colette, Undercover or Sephora to try out products and experiment with looks and then to showcase them on YouTube, Instagram, TikTok or Twitch, and eventually created their own brands and some endeavored later to become celebrity stylists or makeup artists.

There are several implications for brands: an amateur is their own first and best customer, like Pharrell Williams is with his Louis Vuitton menswear collections and Human Race skincare. No one who's ever been in Williams' company failed to notice his ageless look and serene demeanor. A cross between a cultural player and a Buddha, Williams has been a dedicated proponent of sustainability, humanity, health and wellbeing. His latest endeavor doesn't merely reflect Williams' values. They are his values: "We're creating for humans; we're all born in the same skin and Humanrace celebrates this."[5] For brands, this starts with the question: would they buy their own products? Would they believe in their own messaging?

An amateur displays enviable creative flexibility. For brands, this means using their visual and verbal handwriting creatively. Gucci Ghost gave himself the creative freedom of changing the font, format and art of Gucci logo. Kapital, the mecca of the Japanese denim aficionados, features things that only exist in their minds (and in the Kapital store): three leg trousers, wrap-around shirt, a denim apron and more are all there. This creative flexibility generates iconic looks and appeals to collectors' mentality.

Amateurs' production of cultural taste attracts a collective that shares it. For brands, this means putting forward an aesthetic point of view that's attractive to cultural creators and consumers alike. Kanye, Virgil Abloh, Heron Preston, Matthew Williams, and Kim Jones all have a shared style, vocabulary, a way of dressing, music and taste. For amateurs, a collective is a necessary springboard as it includes mentors, role models and reference points.

Amateurs' style creates an imprint on their creative community. For brands, this means having a clearly defined world, ruled by the easy-to-understand principles. Abloh's 3% rule provides a framework for his followers: it's a set of tricks and hacks that lets them practice one's own creativity and fandom. Or merch sprang from streetwear and provided a template for everything from cottagecore to Joe Biden paraphernalia to Demna Gvasalia's collaboration with Apple Music on a merch collection plus a playlist curated by Balenciaga's community.

The entire creative economy is constructed around the amateur. There are mask-selling amateurs (between April and June 2020, $346 million worth of face masks were sold on Etsy), Chinese fansub amateurs, amateur chefs and interior decoration amateurs. Amateurs propelled themselves to the forefront of singing, dancing, fashion design, home makeover and finding a partner.

For a brand to follow an amateur model means both to adopt its behaviors and to treat its audience as amateurs. Far from being trivial, this is where the modern brand power is: amateurs preserve the best of cultural heritage by interpreting it for the present and by making it relevant to those who'd never heard of it. Like culture guides, they tell us what to pay attention to.

Five personas of the creative class

Based on the type of their cultural output they produce, there are five personas of the creative class. All of them are relevant for brands' cultural influence strategy, as they create, circulate, contextualize, package or propagate ideas, objects and language that consumers pay attention to.

Commentators

Commentators are like hired assassins: they don't produce anything themselves, but through their commentary, decide which idea, trend, brand or personality is going to live or die. They are the voice of authority who managed to turn their love for pop culture (and its many niches) into a career. While most commentators focus on one or several favorite genres, they necessarily cast a wide net for their cultural diet since being informed is part of their job. While well-versed in cultural trivia, they prefer the intellectual aspects of cultural analysis and often take a macro perspective on the social and economic significance of the pop culture as a whole. The critic doesn't just pay attention to a subculture, they know who pioneered it, what defines it and how to evaluate contemporary subcultures against the influences that preceded it.

Commentators use culture as a definitive statement about how they relate to the world. For their friends, it's a shared state of mind and the medium through which they connect to others. Often focusing on one or just a few similar subcultures, commentators want to know as much as possible about the people behind the subcultures and taste communities they love. They participate in and sometimes contribute to these communities and regularly attend store openings, book launches, fashion shows, and other events. So regularly in fact, that they often discuss the finer points of events, and probably have an opinion on the "best [insert fashion, music, art, design, film] event ever."

Commentators can often be perceived as the classic smart-ass. They are driven by a strong desire to be first and seek identity via knowledge. They love the obscure and never tire of the trivial one-upmanship that comes with being the world's pop culture know-it-all. Pop culture is the lens through which they see the world and the standard against which they judge themselves and hope to be judged by others; pop culture is inextricably part of who they are. Commentators dabble in all subcultural genres from streetwear to the latest exhibition at the Gagosian and consequently rarely find themselves in a situation without a decisive opinion. They actively seek out new culture creators in hopes of being the first one of their friends in the know.

Curators

Curators are good taste ambassadors: they connect people, products and ideas in a way that creates something that's simultaneously new and familiar – Nike x Dior is an example – and they bridge the gap between different taste communities and introduce them to one another. They also curate design teams. Late Virgil Abloh, a master curator, gave a renewed meaning and purpose in consumers' eyes to everything from IKEA rugs to Evian water. "Virgil was the first African American to be appointed a creative director," says Amy Odell, an author. "These were very hard shoes to fill. Virgil bridged music and fashion in a unique way."[6] For Atlanta de Cadenet Taylor, an entrepreneur and creator, "being a good curator is part of being a successful creative director today. It's a different skill." She mentions Marc Jacobs as a great example: "[He says,] 'I see kids doing this. I cannot do this, so let me find someone who can.'"[7] Enter Ava Nirui, the creative force behind Marc Jacobs's "Heaven" line.

Being a coveted curator of a cultural niche (e.g., menswear, mid-century design, fine dining, music) conveys one's distinction and social standing based on more than posing on a cobblestone street in a selected outfit. It takes taste and knowledge to pick stuff up at Frieze in LA, go to Salone di Mobile in Milan, choose what to wear for Paris Fashion Week or decide whether to eat in Mitte or Osaka or Abu Dhabi.

Knowing where to go and what to do is the currency that, in the modern aspiration economy, makes curators more important than influencers. They guide their audience through culture by putting forward a selection of images, references, codes, product releases or memes. Curation gives even mundane objects value by connecting them with a point of view, heritage, a subculture or purpose that makes them stand out in the vortex of speed, superficiality and newness.

Curators are repositories of specific knowledge, ready to travel the world to obtain a coveted item or experience, and passionately talk about their latest acquisitions. Born in Vancouver, Kevin Ma says he grew up far from the hubs of youth culture. He started Hypebeast as a sneaker blog from his bedroom in 2005. Fast forward to 2019, and the company, now publicly traded and with diversified revenue streams, is the ultimate global destination for streetwear, fashion and culture.

Hypebeast's site enjoys 46 million page views a month and has more than 817,100 Twitter followers and 10.8 million Instagram fans, but Ma's profile is decidedly low. "Curators are often playing the long game, slowly building up knowledge, sharing it, improving upon it," says Colin Nagy, a global brand strategy and marketing lead at Instagram.[8] Because curators are able to focus and dig deep, and because they are highly selective in how they socialize, they regularly build influential cultural niches around themselves – whether that be sneakers or denim or food – and often become a source of inspiration for wider trends. Their identity is often deeply tied to the subject matter, which makes them stand out in the vortex of speed, superficiality and newness.

Creators

Creators strive to put forward original output. Creators can be in the remix, which recontextualizes or puts a personal stamp on already existing creative work; it can be in reissuing the past cultural work; or it can be creating a yet-unseen cultural output.

When they rework the already existing cultural products, creators walk the fine line between imitation (see the following) and creativity. When Amazon allegedly copied Peak Design's Everyday Sling,[9] the bag brand promptly made a video titled "A Tale of Two Slings."[10] When a similar thing happened to Allbirds a year or so ago, they were considerably less amused by it. Down the coast in Silicon Valley, Snap has a "Voldemort" dossier, which documents all of Facebook's aggressive Snapchat feature rip-offs. Now largely forgotten shopping app Spring pioneered years ago a shopping experience that was almost too seamless for its own good. Instagram watched and learned and years later developed its Checkout feature, with a user experience not unlike Spring's. Netflix successfully introduced a completely new business model and viewing experience, only to see itself in stiff streaming competition with HBO, Hulu, Disney and NBC Universal.

Creators have been inspired with each other for decades. What they haven't been absorbing is wisdom. In the contemporary pop culture, winners are those who are able to swiftly peruse a road map laid down by their predecessors to launch, iterate, improve and grow their own creative output and cultural clout.

Most successful modern creators build on top of what's already out there. Late Virgil Abloh was the master of the 3% rule, where he iterated on everything from fashion to automotive design. Brand collaborations are another expression of using the existing creative output and making it slightly different. Both parts are still recognizable but also distinct enough to be considered new.

In creative economy, companies discovered that shunning the new in favor of the incremental has proved to deliver consistent business results. Glossier, with its $1.8 billion valuation, didn't start big. Instead, it gradually evolved from a beauty blog to a single product play to a modern Estée Lauder. Thanks to this slow and steady approach, Glossier amassed 1.5 million potential customers at launch.

Today, millions of Glossier's micro-influencers drive 70% of the company's growth, and everything that Glossier does – from pop-up shops to heavily Instagrammable stores and photo-friendly packaging – is aimed at catering to their social status and influence. Compared to advertising campaigns of established beauty brands, these efforts are low-cost and low-investment. They are a great way for Glossier to evaluate different products (dog toys, anyone?) based on consumer behavior.

These days, in creative industries, customer proximity is the only competitive advantage for businesses. Algorithm-induced commoditization, price transparency and social media-lowered barriers to entry swiped away all the rest. Running apparel brand Tracksmith studied what Nike's been doing, then did the opposite. Instead of projecting the run-until-you-throw-up, elite athlete image, Tracksmith built brand and products around hobbyist runners and "the amateur spirit." The company worked backward from this (growing) target group to create its entire brand around it – and soon became synonymous with well-designed products, vintage aesthetics and a vibrant runner community.

A lot of creators in fashion, luxury, furniture and design industries make money by reissuing the past creative work. *032c*, a cultural publication, calls a tendency to mine the past "the heritage problem," referring to the newly appointed creative directors' habit to look into the archive and redo their brand's iconic history. The tendency may not be, by default, original, but it works. Tiffany & Co. recently launched a creative double-header, a campaign titled "With Love, Since 1837" and the Tiffany Wonder exhibition in Tokyo, both aimed at celebrating this brand's storied past. Kim Jones has been doing something similar since joining Fendi. Gucci, building upon its original Vault idea, launched the story of its loafer, made iconic not only because it is unchanged in time but because it has been a prototype for the Gucci brand.

In the creative economy, the past is the currency. It pushes brands from production of new goods and services toward history, heritage and tradition. In story-mongering, a brand's old output is resurrected and the new output is enriched with motifs from the past in order to give them history. Today, for something to be modern, it needs to be archival.

Unlike the previous economic models that depleted our physical world, the creative economy exploits time. Past is a reliable way of monetizing time (what worked once, is going to work again). "Anything that we are comes from our past," Miuccia Prada recently noted.[11] "There is this discussion of nostalgia, but that's not at all the truth. We look at history to learn something. Taking a piece from the past is not conservative. It's liberating it from its cage." Raf Simons adds, "You cannot talk about beauty without going to the past. You cannot erase the history of beauty, it is what defines our ideas of beauty today. We always go back."[12]

To exploit the past, a brand first needs to have it. If it doesn't, it needs to invent it (see Ralph Lauren[13]). The purpose of inventing heritage and tradition, and their narrative enrichment and embellishment, is to create cultural currency. In the creative economy, cultural currency equals economic currency, and creativity is the mode of its production.

Whoever has the best story, and the best way to tell it, wins. Best stories own time. They get to shape the narrative and define the history (see the movie *The New Look* on Apple TV+).

It's lucrative to own time. As the ultimate currency, time increases price of something. Otherwise, we wouldn't have a saturated resale market. A reboot, a sequel, or a reissue also increases the value and the price of an original. Customers make a purchase with an eye on its future value in the resale markets. Dealers do the same. Thanks to their past, commodities turned investable assets with appreciating value.

In the economy that monetizes time, the ultimate goal is to achieve immortality.

Kering, LVMH and Prada seek immortality through their foundations, which are part of the cultural economy as much as Louvre. Immortality is, however, best achieved when a brand monopolizes one's entire way of passing time. As Patrizio Bertelli formerly of Prada notes, "we want to it be a mindset, an experience centered around the Prada brand . . . Creating an identity that transcends what we sell."[14]

For this transcendence to happen, different areas of cultural production need to fuse. Tourism and branding, film and television, gaming and fashion, art and design, architecture and content creation, and advertising and publishing are becoming a single brand narrative.

Creative production does not aim at originality (it takes time or something truly original to be created, and even more time for it to spread) and is less interested in ideas than in their biography. A biography of an idea, a person or a brand gets dramatized and enriched, and we get Louis Vuitton transformed from a suitcase maker into an artist, Christian Dior into a hero in *The New Look*, and the Gucci family into a heightened drama in *House of Gucci*.

The catch is that the creative embellishment of biographies does not itself stand the test of time. By design, these interpretations are meant to be trendy and constantly replaced by new interpretations of the same heritage and tradition. This is why the members of the creative class who are at the helm of brands – like fashion designers, film directors, hoteliers, writers, luxury CEOs – are getting frequently replaced. To keep going, the creative economy needs interpretative newness.

Interpretative newness makes creative production circular. To get the always new angles, creative production simultaneously traverses separate cultural areas and time through self-reference and copying. In the circular creative production, reboots, sequels and reissues of an origination narrative are the main output. Get ready for Dior Part VII or *The New Look* told through the perspective of a cat.

Despite all of its reverence for the past, the creative economy is ultimately disrespectful of it. The past that the creative economy exploits had once been the future. Originality was such that it broke the confines of its present. Creatives whose biographies we admire always looked forward, never backward. To make creativity immortal, we need to give it a future by bestowing on it enough time to unfold in the present.

Finally, creators also produce a new and yet-unseen cultural output. Most productive creators are proclaimed iconic. In fashion, these are Coco Chanel and then Karl Lagerfeld, Maria Grazia Chiuri, Demna Gvasalia, and until he opted out, Pierpaolo Piccioli. They build their own aesthetic worlds. Daniel Roseberry, a creative director at Schiaparelli, a luxury fashion brand, weaves Schiaparelli story with skill, ease and the confident surrealist lens. Creative and innovative, aesthetes' collections are considered and detail-obsessed; their shows are always narratives that are rich without being excessive or spectacular. Telfar, Thom Browne, Galliano at Margiela, Jonathan Anderson at LOEWE, and Rick Owens are creators. In addition to creators who invent their own aesthetics, there are those who consider creativity through the lens of quality. Nadège Vanhée-Cybulski, a creative director at Hermès, or the late Karl Lagerfeld don't move fast or chase buzz. They create highly coverable iconic products that are in purposefully limited supply.

Imitators

Imitators live at the crossroads of cultural consumption and creation. They are fluent in languages of social media, influence, commentary, creativity, curation and remixing. Their best activity defines how all of these interact. They are turning to pop culture and its many niches for inspiration and for the material they will copy and paste or borrow and repurpose. Imitators revel in choosing the best and the most popular and in their ability to grow and energize their following by disseminating ideas, products and texts created by someone else.

Imitators are more interested in "going viral" than in the content, ideas and products that they put out there since they borrowed them from someone else. They are deeply opportunistic and rush to the front of every parade. Imitators are driven by a strong desire to present them-selves are experts who are in-the-know, without doing the actual work or having the talent to do it. They seek identity via community. Their role in cultural influence strategy is to amplify and widely disseminate the work of others: imitators would literary take anything that will get them more comments, likes and followers.

Hangers-on

Hangers-on are modern groupies, gathering around cool stores, galleries and event spaces and around creators, commentators and curators. Even imitators have a few hangers-on. Hangers-on just want to be included and don't mind spent time and money to do so. They brag about their personal connections with other creative class members, which are usually very distant, and use them to elevate their own importance. They are driven by a strong desire to outwardly demonstrate their membership within a larger cultural group. They seek identity via belonging. Hangers-on are often opportunistic and capitalize on their weak ties with a subculture for personal gains and self-promotion. Hangers-on do not have any marketable culture output – they are the side effect of curators', commentators', critics' and creators' communities.

Notes

1 https://www.amazon.com/Rise-Creative-Class-Revisited-Revised-Expanded/dp/0465042481

2 https://www.amazon.com/Enrichment-Critique-Commodities-Luc-Boltanski/dp/1509528725

3 https://wwd.com/business-news/business-features/aspirational-luxury-consumers-definition-features-clusters-1236272179/

4 Jenkins, Henry, *Textual Poachers*, Routledge, 1992, https://williamwolff.org/wp-content/uploads/2015/01/jenkins-2992-conclusion.pdf

5 Yaptangco, A. (2020, November). Retrieved August 2024, from https://humanrace.com/pages/about-us?srsltid=AfmBOoptgN4YMp_mPiVH2HmLFOTdYsYKuLCTeME6pBlX9RuVyWOdK9Ap

6 Andjelic, A. (2023, March). Retrieved August 2024, from https://www. ssense.com/en-us/editorial/fashion/creative-directors-fashion

7 Andjelic, A. (2023, March). Retrieved August 2024, from https://www. ssense.com/en-us/editorial/fashion/creative-directors-fashion

8 Andjelic, A. (2019, August). Retrieved August 2024, from https://www. fastcompany.com/90397589/personal-branding-for-people-who-hate-personal-branding

9 https://www.theverge.com/2021/3/3/22311574/peak-design-video-amazon-copy-everyday-sling-bag

10 https://www.youtube.com/watch?v=HbxWGjQ2szQ

11 https://www.instagram.com/desigual/p/C4WKw7NtlbQ/

12 Chitrakorn, K. (2024, February). Retrieved August 2024, from https:// www.ft.com/content/a651379c-e2d6-4614-b084-2129cef16aa0

13 https://andjelicaaa.substack.com/p/ralphs-dream

14 Sciorilli Borrelli, S. (2024, March). Retrieved August 2024, from https:// www.ft.com/content/ccb5a32d-be04-45f3-92f5-2b8ffaa0a45b

Conclusion

Why brands need cultural influence strategy

When French sociologist Guy Debord wrote *The Society of Spectacle* in 1967,[1] his goal was to describe, and denounce, the advertising, public relations and celebrity-dictated consumer culture. The premise of Debord's analysis is that "being is replaced by having, and having is replaced by appearing. We no longer live, we aspire, signal, perform."

A June 2023 *New Yorker*'s article,[2] "The Case Against Travel," detailing the performative aspect of modern travel, would agree, but Debord wrote his book before the Internet, suggesting that culture in capitalism – regardless of technology – inevitably leads toward appearances, performance and commodity.

For Bernard Arnault, owner of LVMH, culture is a superstar commodity. Not satisfied with being a mere fashion house, Arnault set his sights on turning Louis Vuitton into a house of culture.

DOI: 10.4324/9781003534907-6

In this, Arnault is not alone. Kering, Prada and Hermès are all bidding for the greatest cultural influence, and with a good reason: in the creative economy, cultural currency equals economic currency, and creativity is the mode of its production. Whoever has the best story, and the best way to tell it, wins. Best stories own time. They get to shape the narrative and define the history (see LVMH's *The New Look*, about Christian Dior).

In the economy that monetizes time, the ultimate goal is to achieve immortality.

Big luxury groups seek immortality through their foundations, which are part of the cultural economy as much as Louvre. Immortality is, however, best achieved when a brand monopolizes one's entire way of passing time. As Patrizio Bertelli, the former CEO of Prada, notes, "we want to it be a mindset, an experience centered around the Prada brand . . . Creating an identity that transcends what we sell."[3]

For this transcendence to happen, different areas of cultural production need to fuse. Tourism and branding, film and television, gaming and fashion, art and design, architecture and content creation, and advertising and publishing are becoming a single brand narrative.

Creativity vs. originality

Cultural products like *Ghostbusters 2*, *Mission: Impossible 17*, the *Barbie* movie, Y2K mood, or Marvel Universe depict capitalism as a deeply uncreative system. Nothing new ever happens: creativity is in curating, reviving and repurposing the past, putting it in new contexts and giving it new interpretations. Originality is not the goal (it takes time for something truly original to be created, and even more time for it to spread), and creativity is less interested in ideas than in their biography. Biography of an idea, a person, or a brand gets dramatized and enriched, and we get Louis Vuitton transformed from a suitcase maker into an artist, Christian Dior into a hero in *The New Look*, and the Gucci family into a heightened drama in *House of Gucci*.

The catch is that the creative embellishment of biographies does not itself stand the test of time. By design, these interpretations are meant to be trendy and constantly replaced by new interpretations of the same heritage and tradition. This is why the members of the creative class who are at the helm of brands – like fashion designers, film directors, hoteliers, writers, and luxury CEOs – are getting frequently replaced. To keep going, the creative economy needs interpretative newness.

Interpretative newness makes creative production circular. To get the always new angles, creative production simultaneously traverses separate cultural areas and time through self-reference and copying. In the circular creative production, reboots, sequels and reissues of an origination narrative are the main output. Get ready for Dior Part VII or *The New Look*, a horror.

Whereas reinterpretation has always been the engine of culture, it used to go in the opposite direction: conventional ideas were recontextualized as radical (a corset in the 1990s, Marc Jacobs artistic collaborations). Today, once-radical ideas are made conventional. Places, times and personalities are all a potential commercial inspiration – a reference: Harlem's history of bootlegging, indie sleaze, Basquiat's art and Keith Haring, whose face can these days be found on a Boss dress.[4]

If modern creativity is in representing the past as new, then the power of that representation rests on celebrity. For Debord, both are commodities: "The celebrity, the spectacular representation of a living human being, embodies the banality of embodying the image of a possible role. Their individuality is sacrificed in order to become a figurehead of the profit-driven system," and "The star is the object of identification with the shallow seeming life that has to compensate for the fragmented productive specializations which are actually lived. Celebrities are commodities themselves."[5] Both the past and celebrity also have proven success rate. The model of reinvention and reappropriation rests on one source code, and its innumerable sequels. There's only one genre in the society of spectacle: the genre of a narrative universe.

Sequels vs. knock-offs

Just like there is Marvel Cinematic Universe, there's Arnault Fashion Universe, with the interconnected set of characters, self-referential narrative lines, and methodical rollouts in categories ranging from hospitality to lifestyle to fashion to travel, making it unnecessary to ever leave it.

Like Marvel's IP, which gives Disney something to do and money to make for decades to come, LVMH's 75 brands provide a nearly-infinite IP. Call Damier, a signature Louis Vuitton print, damouflage and you just gave it a new life; bring back once-popular saddle bag and watch the sales soar.

032c, a cultural criticism magazine, calls this infinite IP capitalization "the heritage problem." The heritage problem refers to the newly appointed creative directors' habit to look into the archive and redo their brand's iconic heritage. The tendency is not, by default, original, but it works. In February 2024 Tiffany & Co., a jewelry retailer, launched a creative double-header, a campaign titled "With Love, Since 1837" and the Tiffany Wonder exhibition in Tokyo, both aimed at celebrating this brand's storied past. Kim Jones has been doing something similar since joining Fendi. Gucci, building upon its original Vault idea, launched the story of its loafer, made iconic not only because it is unchanged in time but because it has been a prototype for the Gucci brand.

In the creative economy, the past is the currency. It pushes brands from production of new goods and services toward history, heritage and tradition. In story-mongering, a brand's old output is resurrected and the new output is enriched with motifs from the past in order to give them history. Today, for something to be modern, it needs to be archival.

Unlike the previous economic models that depleted our physical world, the creative economy exploits time.

The past is a reliable way of monetizing time (what worked once is going to work again). "Anything that we are comes from our past," Miuccia Prada recently noted. "There is this discussion of nostalgia, but that's not at all the truth. We look at history to learn something. Taking a piece from the past is not conservative. It's liberating it from its cage."[6] Raf Simons adds, "You cannot talk about beauty without going to the past. You cannot erase the history of beauty, it is what defines our ideas of beauty today. We always go back."[7]

To exploit the past, a brand first needs to have it. If it doesn't, it needs to invent it, like Ralph Lauren or Häagen-Dazs did. The purpose of inventing heritage and tradition, and their narrative enrichment and embellishment, is to create cultural currency. In the creative economy, cultural currency equals economic currency, and creativity is the mode of its production.

Whoever has the best story, and the best way to tell it, wins. Best stories own time. They get to shape the narrative and define the history (see *The New Look*).

It's lucrative to own time. As the ultimate currency, time increases price of something. Otherwise, we wouldn't have a saturated resale market.[8] A reboot, a sequel or a reissue also increases the value and the price of an original. The endless fashion sequels also create a new dynamic in the market: they turn knockoffs into the most original products around. Not only knockoffs display now-enviable craftsmanship, they also do not pretend to be anything else but the imitation of the original. Spare us the faux references and give us the real replica. Still, customers make a purchase with an eye on its future value in the resale markets. Dealers do the same. Thanks to their past, commodities turned investable assets with appreciating value.

Despite all of its reverence for the past, the creative economy is ultimately disrespectful of it. The past that the creative economy exploits had once been the future. Originality was such that it broke the confines of its present. Creatives whose biographies we admire always looked forward, never backward. To make creativity immortal, we need to give it a future by bestowing on it enough time to unfold in the present.

Parochialism vs. humor

Arnault's cultural ambition is not original. It is also parochial.

"Everything I say is a joke. I am like a caricature of myself, and I like that. It is like a mask," the late Karl Lagerfeld famously said. "And for me the Carnival of Venice lasts all year long."[9]

Lagerfeld was in on his own joke, and this made Chanel irreverent and coveted and unwaveringly relevant. Lagerfeld mastered the art of detournement – or hijacking – the Spectacle by taking it to the extreme and turning it into a caricature. Evian bottle holders, spaceships, icebergs, supermarkets, Choupette – Chanel's Spectacle has been powered by humor, parody, irony and satire.

Today, creative collective MSCHF does something similar, mocking commercial symbolism through its own language. The late Virgil Abloh, referenced surrealists (for some, the last original art form in capitalism) to make fun of the spectacle and then framed his jokes in a museum.

Without a certain lack of respect, brands turn into a dogma. "Waves of enthusiasm for a given product," writes Debord, resemble "moments of fervent exaltation similar to the miracles of the old religious fetishism."[10] Without humor and nuance, brands trivialize the original intention behind their references: bootlegging, subculture, subversion, critique turn into the mainstream, ready-for-sale. What was once an act of subversion and social critique is becomes buttery leather.

So what?

"If I hadn't been in fashion, I would have been in advertising," said Lagerfeld.[11] This attitude was visible in his own comportment as much as in Chanel's weltanschauung. One never knew where the cultural stopped and the commercial started, and that was the point.

In the course of his career, Alexandre de Betak displayed similar sensibility. "My duty is to create a means of expression that will help translate the creations of the fashion designers: to make them be understood and memorized in a moving manner, not just intellectually or conceptually, but also emotionally," Betak says in his book *Betak: Fashion Show Revolution.*[12]

At its best, the Spectacle is a display of design excellence. It sells, wows and communicates the brand image. It is another canvas for brand expression, combining multiple marketing executions into one: event, live-streaming, celebrities and influencers, social media, content, entertainment. Per Betak: "I think that the fashion show as a live event will last a very long time, because people always want to be inspired and encouraged to dream, and there is no limit to all the elements you can employ in a live show – the potential for creativity is boundless."[13]

The Spectacle is the next phase of branding.

In it, the presentation has to be more memorable and relevant than what has been presented; the presentation is the product.

Unlike production of a product, production of a presentation takes all individual contributions and skillsets and mixes them together; individual expertise matters only in function of the presentation.

In the post-industrial economy, this reversal doesn't come as a surprise. Just as capitalism commodified products, rendering them interchangeable, advanced capitalism commodifies experiences and perceptions. Once we ran out of things to produce, we turned toward production of experiences: tourism, sports, fashion.

Luxury has, for long, been excluded from this logic of commodification. Luxury's heritage and cultural role prevented its goods to be perceived as interchangeable; Chanel has a story, Hermès has a story, and Saint Laurent has a story. The business model powering it all is genius: items are sold at steep multiples of the cost of their production.

Arnault did is to take this model to the extreme. In luxury, craftsmanship and branding have always been intertwined; the value of a product was never just craftsmanship (otherwise, we'd be all buying artisanal goods); it was branding (story) plus craftsmanship. Once craftsmanship has been offloaded to China, India or Turkey, luxury is left with branding.

(Not all luxury: Hermès, which still hand-makes its bags in France, does not have a marketing department. But they also say, "We are not luxury. We are high quality.")

Branding as the Spectacle require superior production and performance. A brand's ability to put on a show is how its products are going to be valued and how desirable they will be. Arnault figured out that, in the society of performances, a brand with the highest Spectacle credentials wins. He is also one of the few who can actually afford the Spectacle.

Do not hate the player; hate the game.

As a performance, a recent LV Menswear show has been incredibly successful, with over one billion views.[14] This matters. Performance culture is a culture shaped by performance metrics, including consumer engagement metrics and business metrics. With each consequent Spectacle, a new performance standard is set, and the industry is moving further and further into the branding territory.

This market dynamics introduces a new creative strategy, across luxury fashion organizations. Designers, who first became creative directors, are now producers. Their job is to produce fashion shows, imagery and content, create buzz and grab as much attention as possible.

Those who are unwilling – or unable – to produce Spectacle will have to content themselves with being summoned by the producer to bow at the end of the show.

Those who are will need creative strategy.

A McKinsey study found that companies that prioritize creativity have 67% above-average organic revenue growth and 74% above-average net enterprise value.[15]

Creativity has a superior business value, yet it is too often siloed in "creative" departments, like design or marketing. This is understandable: traditional companies organizationally separate idea generation from idea commercialization.

It also doesn't work anymore.

A lot of creative industries have been forced to accelerate their creative output, in the always-on cadence. Pressure for immediate productivity leads to unremarkable work and is a reason for endless sequels, reissues, archive reboots and self-referencing across creative industries. Productivity pressure also leads to creative directors' short tenures. For the time they are given, creative directors can, at best, offer their interpretation of the brand codes and archives. The newness imperative and the compressed business calendars don't really let them come up with original ideas, much less allow those ideas to grow and mature.

Paired with this creative acceleration is a business pressure to execute and to hit quarterly financial targets. Business performance is designed to be short-term, together with accompanying metrics and expectations of commercial results.

When Pierpaolo Piccioli left Valentino, the fashion industry reacted with a cry for "a need for the intangible, for that magic alchemy that creates and delivers dreams."[16] Tell that to a CFO.

The disconnect is growing between creative industries' need for time to develop and unfold an original idea, which is unpredictable, and a rigid financial calendar that demands predictable financial outcomes. Long-brewing brand desirability goes against the quest for immediate returns. Calvin Klein's Jeremy Allen White campaign from January generated 40 million views on CK's Instagram and drove 85% YoY brand engagement increase. At the same time, Calvin Klein's stock fell 20% and sales in North America dropped 8% YoY.

Turning a brand around takes time, and more than just one campaign.

The disconnect between cultural influence and business results is the result of companies fitting their creative output into the business models that have not changed for decades. In fashion, that means seasonal collections, shows, capsules and special projects. Since improving execution yields an immediate payoff, and creativity doesn't, the focus is on the ever-increasing investments in the existing business models. In fashion, this means the more and more expensive fashion shows.

Demand to deliver great ideas that yield immediate results puts pressure on creative departments, most notably on creative directors. A *Financial Times* March 2024 article, discussing Kering's profit warning, was titled "Sabato de Sarno, the designer who must turn around Gucci."[17]

It is deceivingly simple to look at a newly appointed designer as a brand savior. Designers are part of a complex web of operational, logistical, commercial and strategic decisions. In the past decade, Gucci's strategy has been to target younger, aspirational shoppers at the expense of the older, more price elastic, luxury ones. As a result, Gucci built strong fashion-forward credentials, which were a wind in its sails until the fashion currents changed. This all happened before Sarno's appointment, and the results of both de Sarno's efforts and the efforts of the entire Gucci organization will take a considerable investment of time, money and expertise.

A brand turnaround also requires a creative approach to the organizational transformation. The solution to having the original creative output is to set the business for it.

This does not, mercifully, mean that everyone in the organization needs to be creative (it's OK that financial controllers, for example, are not). It means adopting a creative approach to business opportunities across functions of marketing, merchandising, PR, retail experience, customer service, commercial planning and market growth. It also means having a clear business and brand vision and aligned functional incentives to achieving it, a strong cross-functional leadership that remains their teams of the common brand and business goals, and realistic return on investment and timelines across corporate activities.

Creativity is an approach rather than just the output. As an approach, creativity focuses on business opportunities across corporate functions. As a strategy, creativity marries the process of idea generation and idea commercialization into organizational "middleware."

This middleware combines the role of disorder in the creative industry and strategic rigor of running a business. Creative markets are inherently unpredictable, and this unpredictability has only accelerated. They have a lot less time to come up with, and test, these new ideas. The rules of selling creative products have dramatically changed, as well. Time to market is compressed and companies are often forced to test and try ideas in the world, where they live or die. This forces companies to adopt a portfolio approach: to have a lot of ideas versus just one "big idea" and to capture a lot of cultural moments versus just one "big moment."

The creative industry doesn't need a more efficient execution; it needs more creative responses, processes, and business models.

In particular, this means: In the domain of marketing, creative strategy delivers a lot ideas versus just one "big" idea, and captures a lot of cultural moments versus just one "big moment." Its purpose is to expand a brand's footprint and renew brand associations and provide a stream of always-on entertainment. It tests and tries ideas in the world, where they live or die.

A portfolio approach to idea generation is supported by marketing spend that is considered an investment and a cost of goods sold rather than as an operating expense, an approach that allows them to set realistic expectations on the investment returns. Additionally, creative strategy manages a company's intellectual property, ensuring that brand content and entertainment is consistently monetized.

In addition to monetizable content, creative strategy defines is merch, special editions and capsules, archive reissues and sequels, or awards recognizing an area of culture. It also shapes collaborations outside a brand's original product line, and hospitality properties, like cafes, restaurants, hotels and private experiences.[18]

In the domain of media, creative strategy's job is to develop, launch and synchronize multiple brand signals in culture. This means amplifying a brand's own content through media, in-store experiences and visual merchandising and events, which then become a source of fresh content that is further amplified. Within creative strategy, media spend becomes a creative exercise, which revolves around identification of all the different cultural contexts for a brand to participate in.

Creative approach to media allows a brand to be present across different cultural contexts, be nimble and quickly react if some of these contexts gain momentum (a January 2024 Calvin Klein x Jeremy Allen White campaign is an example).

A way for creative strategy to ensure that a brand is present in a number of cultural contexts is to use frequent creative collaborators (and amplify their creative output through its media buys), as these creators bring their fandom with them. Other ways are seeding of merch, amplified through media, as well as events, sponsored content and affiliates.

Creative strategy uses media for interstitial storytelling, which refers to a series of mini-stories that are connected into a web of a wider narrative.

Creative strategy defines the cadence of messaging to mimic movie releases, through teasers, trailers, marketing activations, merch, events and launches. The role of creative strategy in media is to build anticipation around new product releases.

Creative strategy's job is to amplify brand in culture with an experimental, portfolio approach to all brand actions, creation of cultural characters, moments of interest, entertainment production, and fandom building.

Creative strategy considers the entire funnel, though content, messaging, commercial planning, community building and membership programs, events and social media, personalization and specialized retail services. Creative strategy marries short-term sales goals and long-term gains in brand awareness, affinity, consideration, advocacy and loyalty.

In the domain of merchandising, creative strategy makes sure that there's a narrative around the assortment and a synchronization between the annual brand and product story. Creative strategy details the product drip cadence to provide novelty and interest.

Additionally, creative strategy in merchandising provides the full look options and wear scenarios, styling guides and lookbooks. It puts brand personas front and center, making sure that the product assortment appeals to different target customer groups, creating many doors into the brand. It also defines merch to accompany product collections.

Creative strategy ensures that merchandising plays a pivotal role in the brand's creative universe and that it strategically integrates archives, hero products, capsules and collaborations with the main collection into one consistent brand world. It also ensures strategic newness of the assortment, and manages demand volatility. It links in-season assortment flexibility with marketing and creative output.

In the domain of design, creative strategy ensures a consistent implementation of a signature brand aesthetic. Clearly defined brand aesthetics is how a brand participates in culture and is told through product design, fashion direction and styling.

Creative strategy also defines the annual fashion direction and its seasonal rollout, choses archival revivals, vintage curation, special editions and collaborations.

Creative strategy defines celebrity (hero) products for a brand. For example, Millionaire Speedy is meant to create halo around all (non-millionaire) LV's Speedys. Those who have a Millionaire Speedy, though, know that everyone else knows how much they spent on it. The role of a brand's hero products is to be the purest distillation of the brand identity and values, a bridge between the brand heritage and its future, and the fodder for brand collaborations. Burberry trench, Calvin Klein briefs, Stanley Cup and Gucci loafers are some of the examples of hero products. Hero products are the purest distillation of the brand identity and values and are a bridge between the brand heritage and its future. They are foundations of a brand's product pyramid and fodders for a brand's collaborations. They present the building blocks of customers' wardrobe and, like Avengers, represent the brand in the material culture.

Creative strategy also defines the product pyramid and ensures that it works for the entire range of customer personas. At the top, there are capsules and collaborations, and at the bottom is trend-driven assortment. Pricing strategy and product quality reflect this pyramid, with capsules and collaborations featuring elevated fabrics and design.

In the domain of retail, creative strategy defines the product experience in digital and physical retail. Visual handwriting is present through windows display but also through the color palette, styling, product assortment selection, sales and promotional panels design, and selection of the seasonal campaign imagery.

Brand and seasonal lookbooks and styling guide both customers and sales associates about the brand look. Websites and stores are synchronized through creative strategy in their visual and user experience design, consistent and recognizable as belonging to a single brand. In physical retail, the brand designs pop-ups and events, and on the website, it is in charge of art direction for e-commerce, email copy and CRM programs design and copy.

In the domain of customer service, creative strategy spends more on data scientists. It adopts customer-first view in product design, merchandising, media, retail and marketing communication, and it recognizes that a collection launch, a store opening, a website redesign, or a campaign launch is just the beginning of a process of obtaining marketplace feedback, and a base for ongoing growth.

In the domain of business, creative strategy incorporates promotional calendar into the annual sales and revenue goals, and ties is to cultural initiatives and marketing calendar. It also explores new business models, like Moncler Genius, Phoebe Philo's drop model cadence of new product releases through her own website, and Telfar's bag security program. Creative strategy's job is to keep making creative output accountable in terms of business results, as well as to keep commercial and marketing planning work closely together. It has a holistic approach, and ensures that all corporate functions work in sync toward the same goal.

Creativity-driven business transformation

Traditional fashion business model revolves around designers staging presentations of their work for buyers and media. With the increasing number of annual presentations, this model has been stretched to its limits. The solution has so far been to make this model more efficient and the shows more spectacular and expensive, with diminishing returns. This winners-take-all scenario makes the already-big fashion players bigger, at the expense of smaller, emerging and new designers and brands. (An often-quoted example of this kind of obliviousness is Kodak, which kept making the process of manufacturing and distributing chemical-based film more efficient instead of figuring out how to adapt to digital photography. Blockbuster is another example, and the entire media industry is yet another.)

Instead of making the current fashion business model more efficient, it is better to spread the pressure for innovation, novelty and profit from designers and design departments to everyone else. When designers are not given enough time to develop constant innovation, then making the innovation process more distributed among functions can help.

Instead of a single product, innovation in fashion is now a matter of producing a creative stack. Just like entertainment companies produce an entertainment stack around their creative output (including marketing, distribution, events, PR, activations, merch, etc.), fashion's creative stack consists of the product and the innovative ways of bringing it to market.

Marketing, distribution, merchandising, retail experience, merch and PR are not anymore separate from collections; they are part of the same stack, and custom-made for each. This requires creative collectives in place of siloed organizations, lateral collaboration instead of top-down management, and distributed instead of centralized creativity. Outside of fashion, MSCHF is an example of this kind of creative organization; the frequency and originality of their output has so far been impressive. Their releases are organized like a creative stack: the product is combined with its marketing, distribution and sales.

No single individual can come up with the completely, original, imaginative ideas every six months, consistently, for years. But a whole group of people might.

Being innovative in merchandising, communication, PR, store design and experience, social media, community building and nurturing fandom requires a radical rethinking of fashion talent and its organization, and a redefinition of the corporate functions and processes. The fashion industry has a set of new challenges to address, and they require the same innovative, creative, passionate and curious way it takes to design a dress or a coat.

For companies to execute their cultural influence strategy, there are three corporate mindset shifts that need to happen first:

Marketing is creative production. Traditional brand marketing toolkit (TV and print advertising, OOH and PR) has been replaced by brands making cultural products. This is a shift from strategy to the execution and from a couple of big ideas to a lot of small ones that are tested in the real world. Jacquemus' creative production unifies fun products (double-heeled strappy sandals), fun bits of content (Instagram), fun art direction, fun retail experience and fun stunts. Casablanca similarly produces an upbeat and joyful world, where brand products are part of the experience and a lifestyle. Creative production's job is to keep creating, synchronizing and amplifying cultural products on an ongoing basis and throughout the entire funnel.

Spread financial accountability. Brand, business and product always go together. When there is a closer collaboration between marketing, business, merchandising, sales, product, and customer experience, accountability for financial results is distributed among all of them. Financial ownership is shared. Creative production also ensures that all functions are part of the same production process, that they amplify each other, and that they all work toward the same financial results. Creative production links commercial and cultural influence actions closely together and allows for the long-term approach to brand investments.

Creativity beats efficiency. Companies are well-versed in streamlining operations, cutting costs, increasing speed, and reducing employee count. But, while companies may be set up for efficiency, efficiency is not going to give them competitive advantage. Creativity is – in processes, business models, organizational design, and approaches to responding to economic and social shifts. Within the creative approach to the business problem-solving, cultural influence strategy is an investment rather than operating expense, allowing companies to set realistic expectations on their returns.

Brand, product and business go together

Creativity-driven business transformation works only when all corporate functions are in sync. In retail, this means strategically integrating brand, product and business in the manner described in the following.

On March 13, 2024, Inditex (owner of Zara, Massimo Dutti, Oysho, Pull & Bear, Bershka and Stradivarius) reported their 2023 net profit. It was the highest ever, with a 10.4% sales jump to 39.1 billion USD, per Reuters. Zara, the world's biggest fashion retailer, contributed most to these results. Per Inditex CEO, this growth was the result of strong sales, selling more clothes at higher prices, logistics expansion and opening new distribution centers, improving online platforms and expanding its store space.

Zara's uninterrupted rise is the result of three factors: a clearly defined business strategy, a clearly defined product strategy, and a clearly defined brand strategy.

Business strategy refers to clear and measurable annual sales, margins, revenue and profit objectives and the ways to reach them through pricing, demand forecasting, channel allocation, distribution segmentation and overall inventory planning. Business strategy also monitors retail channels performance, individually and together, and defines cross-channel amplification. It takes into account competitor moves, consumer behavior trends, and macro-economic conditions. Finally, it defines strategic investments in technology, new categories and retail channels.

Product strategy refers to the product pyramid; fashion direction and product design; management of fabrics, materials and suppliers; pricing; and merchandising and assortment planning.

Brand strategy refers to consistent delivery of the promise that a brand made to customers and to reinforcement of the reason that a company exists in the world. It covers creative and art direction, styling and visual merchandising, cultural influence and PR, marketing strategy and media planning, commercial planning and customer relationship management – all of which ideally create and convey a distinct and recognizable brand world.

Underpinning the three is operational excellence throughout the entire value chain. (A combination of a successfully executed three factors is most visible in the store experience: I was impressed by Zara's new flagship on the Avenue des Champs-Élysées on my recent trip to Paris).

The mix of business, product and brand creates and maintains sales momentum, profit and growth. Just like a stool cannot stand without all three legs, a company cannot succeed if one or two of the strategies are dysfunctional, underperforming or nonexistent.

Business

A good business strategy is clear, long-term, nimble and consistently executed. It provides short-term goals and a long-term vision. It is measurable and sets clear priorities.

Zara's pricing strategy, channel allocation, distribution segmentation and assortment planning, paired with superior data-driven demand forecasting, provided a winning combination of "who to sell to," "where to sell" and "how to market their products." This combination is constantly tested via Zara's superior data and analytics capabilities that allow it to swiftly react to customer demand across different markets and modify supply.

Zara's retail channels – physical stores, website, app and social media – are all mutually integrated in what comes the closest that I have seen of an omnichannel approach. Self-checkout in Zara stores is powered by its app, which collects customer shopping data from all channels. A recently launched Zara Hair category is shoppable on Instagram.

Customer experience in stores, through e-commerce and on the app has a seamless, intuitive, engaging and elevated UX. The experiences are aligned and consistent and conveys one brand.

Zara's customer strategy is bifurcated. Zara's assortment services its core, trend-chasing, deal-seeking customer, but its Studio Collections,

Capsules (e.g., Steven Meisel), and collaborations attract the premium, more discerning and less price-sensitive customer, as well as add aspirational dimension to the core customer purchases. Getting a $29 turtleneck feels more aspiring with Sasha Pivovarova's editorial next to it.

Zara is driven by a clear and strategic business mission to "give customers what they want and get it to them faster than anyone else." It hits on two core sources of Zara's competitiveness: speed of trends and speed to market. The former has to do with understanding of culture; the latter with flexible and data-driven supply chain. The mission is Zara's North Star in all its business decisions, from selection of suppliers to logistics and distribution to sales.

Finally, Zara's business model is a hybrid between fast retail and luxury strategy. From fast retail, it takes novelty, trend responsiveness and speed. From luxury strategy it takes limited edition capsules and collaborations, elevated retail experience across channels, and fashion's most exclusive talent.

For 2024 and 2025, Zara's clear priorities are logistics, customer experience (live-streaming) and store network expansion. There is a set annual budget and success metrics for this business growth strategy (so far, the YoY sales results have been positive).

Product

Zara's product pyramid works for its wide customer range. At the top are capsules and collaborations, and at the bottom is trend-driven assortment. Pricing strategy and product quality reflect this pyramid, with capsules and collaborations featuring elevated fabrics and design. In the past few years, Zara featured Charlotte Gainsbourg and Kaia Gerber collections, Peter Lindbergh merch, and collaborations with Stephen Meisel, Studio Nicholson, Harry Lambert and Ader Error, among others. These frequent collaborations and capsules give halo to the entire product pyramid

In terms of merchandising, Zara mastered the speed of open to buy to deliver the constant assortment newness and trendiness to its core customer. It has also built its inventory management around contracted product life spans and increased demand volatility. Before anyone else, Zara moved toward in-season assortment flexibility, including adding fast-tracked products and near-shoring. All of this allows Zara to predict demand patterns, accelerating its time to market.

Zara's pricing strategy, which in recent years has seen price increases faster than H&M, aligns prices with value perception and uses analytics to price elasticity and margin dynamics.

The brand's 300+ design team employs a mix of the top fashion talent and "ghost designers," who, like ghost writers, churn out hits without revealing their name.

Brand

A couple of years ago, there were short films of Chloë Sevigny in a bubble bath on the Zara website. The site also featured Fabien Baron Zara Tribute curation of Peter Lindberg's photography, with merch to match. This March, Zara released its new studio collection, titled Rêverie, photographed by Steven Meisel, who also designed one of the brand capsules in the fall of 2023.

The creative universe that Zara has been meticulously building over the past five-plus years is discerning, elevated, and consisting of the fashion's top talent. Steven Meisel and Fabian Baron join models Kaia Gerber, Sasha Pivovarova, Marisa Berenson, Jessica Stam and Edie Campbell, among others.

This creative universe does not come cheap, and years of persistent brand investment and the corresponding brand creative spend to elevate Zara's brand image paid off, as its net profit shows. Site photography, social media and stores are never not modern, never not cutting-edge fashion, and never not making products extremely desirable through the mix of clever art direction and different media formats. Zara is also mercifully devoid of nostalgia.

The outcome is that everyone wears Zara. Stores are always packed; there are lines before its opening hours. Zara app is one of the few retail brand apps that I use. We have all been primed to go and see "what's new," and we know that we will always find it, at a great value. Zara mastered shopping as entertainment and the "everything fashion store" positioning for our different wardrobe needs. It is worn together with luxury brands.

It is extraordinarily naive to think that a brand revamp alone can transform the fate of a retailer. It is like putting a lipstick on a pig. Changing the brand expression without changing the underlying business and operational practices never yields results. As Zara examples shows, though the years-long series of strategic business, product, operational and brand decisions, the company successfully grew into the world's top retailer with elevated brand positioning, desirable and relevant product offering, consistent business growth, and enviable operational excellence. There's a lesson here for all retailers.

Linking cultural influence to financial impact

When selecting their strategy of cultural influence, brands need to first define their short- and long-term goals, their investment in achieving these goals, and their expected return on this investment. Then they should select the strategy of cultural influence that is best going to deliver their expected ROI.

A big part of the process of selecting the strategy of cultural influence is to assign KPIs to its three components: (a) story, (b) cultural products and (c) media amplification. The role of these KPIs is to:

- Define impact that the selected strategy of cultural influence has on revenue.

- Define financial contributions from each of the cultural products and cultural amplification tactics.

- Justify a given investment in particular cultural products and their media amplification.

- Work toward predictive and/or retrospective scenarios that link brand actions with financial performance.

- Manage creativity for profit and growth.

Brand story is operationalized through cultural products and media amplification tactics. It is measured through success of the narrative rollout, selection of cultural products, media amplification mix, and audience segmentation strategy. Each of the cultural products are amplified with a specific audience, through the specific media tactics that range from mass to niche. Each has a goal and a KPI assigned as well as the contribution to the overall financial results, as described in Figure 1.1.

The new cultural influence funnel looks as shown in Figure 1.2. Connecting cultural products with media amplification tactics and audiences, accompanied with the goals and KPIs, allows a brand to link its cultural influence strategy with financial results and is an improvement compared to the traditional brand marketing approach and metrics.

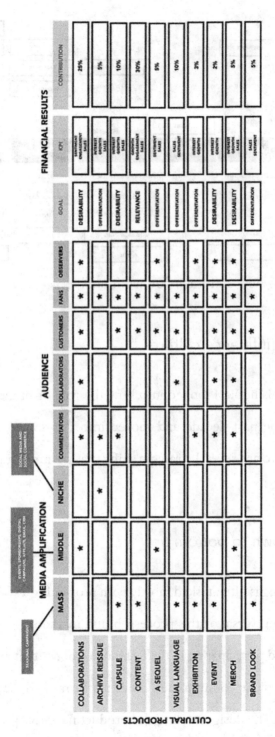

Figure 1.1 Cultural products, media amplification, audience and KPIs

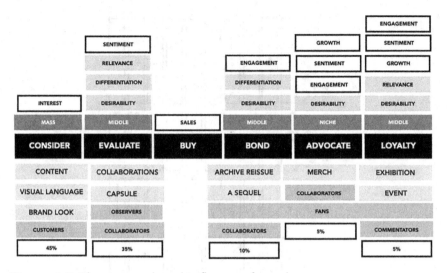

Figure 1.2 The new cultural influence funnel

How brands influence culture

Throughout this book, I looked into how the role of brand marketing expanded in the past decade and moved into the domain of cultural influence. There are several strategic shifts that position brands to start making culture.

From top down to bottom up

Brand marketing is often tasked mostly with promoting a seasonal brand collection. In a reversal of this process, brand marketing is tasked with recognizing and participating in the fashion aesthetics that are emerging in subcultures, niche communities, resale platforms and/or around pop culture events. The design, styling and product narrative process is now bottoms up, with coastal grandma, Barbiecore, or dark academia originating with the customer. Key tactics: creator collaborations, fan and community management, content and curation.

From advertising to entertainment

For Gen Z, shopping is the top among their entertainment activities (above playing video games). Modern brands are in the business of entertainment, and in addition to seasonal campaigns, the job of brand marketing is to provide quirky and fun snippets of always-on content, merch and products, and creative collaborations that introduce novelty and to plan its seasonal campaigns as entertainment products, like movies, through teasers, trailers, opening nights and launches. This is the opposite of how traditional brand marketing works, where it is released at the same time as the collection. Instead, the collection needs to be teased through content and merch prior its launch to drive interest. For Jacquemus, SSENSE and Gstaad Guy, the tone of voice and visual language are joke-y and insider-y, the same as one would speak with their friends. Key tactics: content, events and creative partnerships.

From audience to fans

The fastest way to attract new brand fans is to activate its already existing fans and let them do the word-of-mouth work. Vintage purchases are aspirational, as they let customers flex their curatorial and environmental muscles. Vintage finds are rare and one of a kind, providing symbolic differentiation that new brand products cannot. Gucci Vintage, a new venture from Gucci, replacing its Vault initiative, is a case in point: vintage items sold at Gucci's vintage auctions reach multi-times prices of new items. Key tactics: archives.

From cutting through the noise to making noise

Anything that MSCHF does is simultaneously a stunt and a perfect cultural commentary, smart enough to recognize the zeitgeist and make fun of it. MSCHF's collaborations with Tiffany, Crocs, and a slew of unofficial ones, all got the culture talking. So did JW Anderson's pigeon bag, Casablanca Nicolas Cage ads, Loewe Maggie Smith ads, and Schiaparelli faux taxidermy. The precursor of it all was Marc Jacobs, who changed Louis Vuitton logo immediately after joining the brand (and being told that the only thing that he cannot change is logo). Key tactics: brand and product iconography, graphic design, collaborations.

From promotion to collaboration

Traditionally, brand marketing was entrusted with promoting a company's identity and values. By opening up interpretation of this identity and values, a brand ensures its own longevity and future: just like the most enduring cultural stories and sagas are those that are oral, transported from generation to generation, with community additions and embellishments, so the most enduring brand stories are those that are built with a community: through creative partnerships, collaborations and creative influences. Key tactics: partnerships and collaborations, special editions and capsules.

From products to the look

Brand marketing is often tasked with touting product benefits in addition to brand storytelling. Product focus is today less important than all of the ways this product can be used, worn, and interacted with. More important than a skirt or a pair of boots is how they come together, thanks to TikTok and Instagram, where people buy from other people, get inspired by them and emulate their style. This makes seeding products into different cultural niche communities even more important, as a brand never knows which styling is going to win. Styling additionally immediately provides wear scenarios, as well as infinite narrative opportunities to connect products with subcultures, pop culture, current events and conversations. Key tactics: content, personas, wear scenarios.

From attention to emotion

"To sell something surprising, make it familiar; and to sell something familiar, make it surprising,"[19] noted Raymond Loewy, the father of industrial design. The most visually arresting items from the past couple of years – Pharrell's damouflage, JW Anderson's pigeon bag, and Schiaparelli faux taxidermy are simultaneously surprising and familiar. The emotional resonance that accompanied all of Virgil Abloh's projects, from branding Evian to IKEA rugs is due to their symbolic value that rested on his 3% rule. Instant recognizability met novelty. When ALD started collaborating with New Balance, he took beloved '70s and '80s classics and made them just enough new for 2020s. Matthieu Blazy's "perverse banality" – turning the most basic objects, like a T-shirt or a pair of jeans into pinnacles of craftsmanship, known only to the wearer, is an example of this trend, as is Bottega's celebration of the "ordinary." Key tactics: graphic design, visual language, repeatable narrative anchors, interstitial storytelling, sequels and reboots.

From celebrity person to celebrity product

Stanley has been in business for more than a century. Cue in TikTok, and the recent mayhem of Stanley Cup product desirability put its sales projections to $750 million in 2023. In addition to products that, like Stanley Cup, experience a sudden burst in popularity thanks to social media influence, brands today need to have products they are known and recognized for, together with a unique narrative to go with.

Gucci loafer is so notorious, notoriously recognized, and rich in symbolism, that Gucci rooted its entire collection in it (it was when Gucci was in-between designers, so the loafer was also a symbol of resilience and unity). A brand's hero products are the purest distillation of the brand identity and values (ESPRIT has eight) and are a bridge between the brand heritage and its present and future. They are foundations of a brand's product pyramid and fodders for a brand's collaborations. They present the building blocks of customers' wardrobe and, like Avengers, represent the brand in the material culture. Key tactics: hero products, content, personas, collaborations.

From awareness to awareness + retention

As brand marketing moves to cover the entire funnel, its executions need to retain customers as much as they attract them. Merch and collaborations are the best way of doing this, as customers get immediately something tangible, enriched with the cultural capital. Merch and collaborations are immediately inserted into the cultural exchange system, which automatically retains customers through associations and symbolic value. Key tactics: collabs and merch.

From top of funnel to the entire funnel

Traditionally, brand marketing is focused on top of funnel actions and KPIs (awareness, interest, consideration). It overemphasizes "consider" and "buy" stages of the customer journey, with allocation of the most of media resources to building preference pre-purchase. The result is often deadlock in customer base. The new brand marketing focuses on the entire funnel, making "evaluate" and "advocate" stages more relevant through content, collaborations, merch, curation and creative partnerships. Media investment moves toward continuous brand presence throughout the entire customer journey (membership rewards, private and invite-only events, customization, styling, and early access services, exclusive content) versus just building preference pre-purchase. Key tactics: membership clubs, personalization, retail experience.

From cost center to revenue driver

By capitalizing on its own intellectual property, brand marketing turns from cost center to revenue driver. Revenue comes from brand content and entertainment that is independently monetized, like the *Michelin Guide*. The *Michelin Guide* started in Clermont-Ferrand in 1889 as a way for the Michelin tire company to encourage more tourists to take car trips (and wear their tires off), at the time when there were less than 3,000 cars in France. The guide originally included information like maps, tire-changing and fuel-filling manuals, and rest stops, but over time it started including lists of hotels and restaurants. The Michelin categorization of restaurants became exceedingly popular, and the company hired mystery diners (food critics) to anonymously dine in and review restaurants, assigning them stars. In addition to monetizable content, there is merch, special editions and capsules, archive reissues and sequels, awards recognizing an area of culture, collaborations outside a brand's original product line, and hospitality properties, like cafes, restaurants, hotels and private experiences. Key tactics: collaborations, experiential retail, pop-ups, content, special editions, merch.

Finally, in the narrative universe-building approach, the entire new brand marketing toolkit comes together: archives, hero products, content, capsules, collaborations, product reboots and sequels, branded experiences and experiential retail, merch, styling and events. Each of these creative executions amplifies and augments one another, and synchronized, they together create a frequency in culture. Graphic design, visual language, brand and product iconography, and repeatable narrative anchors all create consistency and are the foundation for experimentation with external creators, collaborators, and partners. They are all tactics in a brand's cultural strategy.

Brands used to influence popular culture through their advertising on mass media like TV, print, billboards, or public relations. Today, they influence culture through the cultural products they create: content, merchandising, events, aesthetics, experiences, archives, history, entertainment and fandom. These cultural products are directed to subcultures, taste communities and consumer niches. Through these cultural products, brands tell their story. Cultural products, and, by proxy, the brand story are amplified through media. Once they manage to influence culture, companies grow their business. Brands and businesses with significant cultural influence command higher prices, capture greater market share, avoid commodification, maintain advantage over competition, and enjoy customer loyalty.

Cultural influence strategy is less about communicating (just) the brand identity and values and more about activating this identity and values as a consistent, encompassing and entertaining brand world that people aspire to be part of and identify with.

To get there, company leadership should avoid hiring mass influencers, working with the same celebrities every other brand is working with, slapping their sponsorships on cultural events without giving these sponsorships legs and scale in the form of the fully-fledged marketing program that connects all aspects of the brand with this sponsorship, and investing money in marketing without assigning specific KPIs to this investment.

Instead, they should give themselves longer time horizons to establish cultural relevance; start measuring financial impact of their brand actions; diversify their cultural products beyond campaigns and advertising, and connect them into one narrative universe; and really care about a subculture, and contribute to it, rather than just capitalize on it.

Culture is a big business. It is also a big social and economic commentator and critic. Culture tells us what we need to know about the world we live in and about what we should pay attention to and why. The strategy of cultural influence is the same.

Notes

1 Debord, Guy, The Society of Spectacle, Black & Red, 1970, https://www.amazon.com/Society-Spectacle-Guy-DEBORD/dp/0934868077

2 https://www.newyorker.com/culture/the-weekend-essay/the-case-against-travel

3 Sciorilli Borrelli, S. (2024, March). Retrieved August 2024, from https://www.ft.com/content/ccb5a32d-be04-45f3-92f5-2b8ffaa0a45b

4 https://www.hugoboss.com/us/boss-x-keith-haring-dress-in-printed-tulle/621384865759.html

5 Andjelic, A. (2023, July). Retrieved August 2024, from https://andjelicaaa.substack.com/p/the-society-of-spectacle

6 Chitrakorn, K. (2024, February). Retrieved August 2024, from https://www.ft.com/content/a651379c-e2d6-4614-b084-2129cef16aa0

7 Chitrakorn, K. (2024, February). Retrieved August 2024, from https://www.ft.com/content/a651379c-e2d6-4614-b084-2129cef16aa0

8 https://www.retaildive.com/news/resale-secondhand-apparel-market-growth-projections/711476/#:~:text=Of%20the%20%2443%20billion%20U.S.,an%20average%20of%2011%25%20annually

9 Fisher, L. A. (2020, February). Retrieved August 2024, from https://quotefancy.com/quote/847046/Karl-Lagerfeld-I-am-like-a-caricature-of-myself-and-I-like-that-It-is-like-a-mask-And-for

10 Andjelic, A. (2023, July). Retrieved August 2024, from https://andjelicaaa.substack.com/p/the-society-of-spectacle

11 Fisher, L. A. (2020, February). Retrieved August 2024, from https://www.brainyquote.com/quotes/karl_lagerfeld_472579

12 De Betak, Alexadre, Betak: Fashion Show Revolution, Phaidon Press, 2017, https://www.amazon.com/Betak-Fashion-Show-Revolution-Alexandre/dp/0714873535

13 Andjelic, A. (2023, July). Retrieved August 2024, from https://andjelicaaa.substack.com/p/the-society-of-spectacle

14 https://theneptunes.org/2024/05/pharrells-louis-vuitton-show-draws-over-1-billion-views/#:~:text=ByMika&text=Pharrell's%20Louis%20Vuitton%20debut%20show,300%20Million%20from%20press%20accounts

15 https://www.mckinsey.com/capabilities/mckinsey-digital/our-insights/creativitys-bottom-line-how-winning-companies-turn-creativity-into-business-value-and-growth

16 Zargani, L. (2024, March). Retrieved August 2024, from https://wwd.com/fashion-news/designer-luxury/valentino-future-pierpaolo-piccioli-alessandro-michele-1236285209/

17 Klasa, A., & Sciorilli Borrelli, S. (2024, March). Retrieved August 2024, from https://www.ft.com/content/638d4587-81d7-4d9e-bd40-2e636ce18523

18 https://www.harpersbazaar.com/uk/fashion/what-to-wear/a60254609/luxury-fashion-in-store-experiences/?utm_source=substack&utm_medium=email

19 Thompson, D. (2017, February). Retrieved August 2024, from https://www.theatlantic.com/magazine/archive/2017/01/what-makes-things-cool/508772/

Index

Note: Page numbers in *italics* indicate figures

Printed in the United States
by Baker & Taylor Publisher Services